Wayne A. R. Leys is Professor of Philosophy at Southern Illinois University. He received his Ph.D. degree from the University of Chicago in 1930. His books include *Ethics and Social Policy, Ethics for Policy Decisions,* and *Philosophy and the Public Interest.* He has written articles appearing in such journals as *Public Administration Review, Annals of the American Academy of Political and Social Science, Antioch Review, Journal of General Education,* and *Physics Today.*

P. S. S. Rama Rao is Assistant Professor of Philosophy at Miami University, Oxford, Ohio. He is a graduate of the University of Delhi and received his Ph.D. degree in 1968 from Southern Illinois University. His articles have appeared in *The Aryan Path, Legal and Moral Obligation,* and in several Indian journals. He was assistant to the editor in the preparation of *The Philosophy of C. I. Lewis* and the reprinting of *The Philosophy of G. E. Moore.*

K. L. Shrimali is Vice-Chancellor at the University of Mysore in India. He was Visiting Professor of Educational Administration and Foundations at Southern Illinois University in 1968.

N. A. Nikam is President of the Indian Philosophical Congress, and former Vice-Chancellor of the University of Mysore in India. He is currently (1969) Visiting Professor of Philosophy at Southern Illinois University.

GANDHI
and America's Educational Future

An Inquiry at
Southern Illinois University

WAYNE A. R. LEYS

and

P. S. S. RAMA RAO

FOREWORD BY K. L. SHRIMALI
EPILOGUE BY N. A. NIKAM

Southern Illinois University Press
Carbondale and Edwardsville
Feffer & Simons, Inc.
London and Amsterdam

Publication of this volume has been made possible
by a special grant from the University

Printed in the United States of America
Designed by Gary Gore
Standard Book Number 8093-0388-4

Library of Congress Catalog Card Number 76-83662

Foreword

THE GANDHI Centennial Committee of the Southern Illinois University has undertaken several projects in connection with the celebration of Gandhi Centennial on October 2, 1969. The most significant project taken up by this Committee is to bring out a publication on the "Educational Responses to Gandhi." In this scholarly work Professor Wayne A. R. Leys and Dr. P. S. S. Rama Rao have shown that Gandhi's teachings have some relevance even for the highly industrialised American society. There is no dearth of literature on Gandhi but this study breaks new ground and I am sure will be of immense interest both in the U.S.A. and India.

Gandhi was neither a philosopher nor a political scientist. It is vain to find any systematic philosophy or political theory in his teachings. The modern man living in a highly industrialised society may find many contradictions in Gandhi's thought and teachings. What is then the secret of Gandhi's greatness? He was called "*Mahatma*" (Great Soul) because he was in line with those sages and saints of India for whom the pursuit of truth or self realisation became the highest goal. His life dedicated to the pursuit of Truth more than his teachings moved millions of his countrymen and would continue to be a source of inspiration to people all over the world.

Gandhi's greatest strength was his *Dharma* (righteousness). By following the path of *Dharma*, he was able to fight against social injustice, religious fanaticism and political tyranny. Through his personal example he has demonstrated to the world that it is only by following the path of *Dharma* (righteousness) that man can triumph over the forces of darkness and falsehood. Evil must be resisted, said Gandhi, not with Evil but with Good. This is the essence of Gandhian teachings.

2033 いひ

The United States which is one of the most powerful nations of the world has tremendous responsibility for reducing tension and for maintaining peace in the world. In this nuclear age it is now clear that man must find some other alternative to war as a means for resolving conflicts if human race is to be saved from catastrophe. Gandhi has shown us the way. His ideas and teachings bore good fruits in Indian soil since they found an echo in the hearts of millions of his countrymen. The voice of truth and nonviolence that was spoken by Gandhi has been spoken in India by great spiritual leaders for centuries. It may not sound the same sympathetic chord in the hearts of other people belonging to a different civilization. But since the Gandhian thought gives some hope to the war weary world it needs serious consideration by our generation which has the power to annihilate the human race and also the resources to relieve the distress of the suffering humanity. From this point of view, this study which attempts to examine how the Gandhian thought can help in resolving the conflicts and contradictions which face the American society today assumes special significance. It is my sincere hope that it would be widely read by the educators all over the world.

Carbondale, Illinois
December 12, 1968

K. L. Shrimali, *Vice Chancellor*
University of Mysore, India

Preface

In the spring of 1967 the Indian students at Southern Illinois University proposed that the University participate in the world-wide observance of the centennial of Gandhi's birth, October 2, 1969. A number of American students and professors expressed willingness to participate. After several meetings the Centennial Committee was organized under the chairmanship of Dean Clarence Hendershot and two subcommittees began work: one concerned with the planning of campus events under the chairmanship of Herbert Marshall and a second committee looking into the possibility of publishing a book. This volume is the product of the latter committee's efforts.

At first it was thought that a *Festschrift*, a symposium consisting of scholarly essays, might deal with the impact of Gandhi upon the West. This seemed promising because, at that time, Martin Luther King was in the headlines with an avowedly Gandhian campaign for Negro rights. But it soon developed that some of the committee members, who had first-hand knowledge of India and who had thought a great deal about nonviolent civil disobedience, were not sure that they had anything to say that had not been said over and over again in the immense literature of Gandhiana. The Southern Illinois University Library had an unusually large collection of this literature, thanks to the interest and diligence of the late Professor William Henry Harris. And it did not require much sampling of this collection to convince us that writings about Gandhi tended to be repetitious of a few themes and often hortatory rather than analytic.

Accordingly, the Committee decided, during the winter of 1967–68, to try something different. Instead of inviting

vii

scholars to contribute essays concerning Gandhi's challenge
to the West, the Committee would prepare a document and ask
people in different disciplines to comment on the document.
Such a document was prepared and released a few days after
the assassination of Martin Luther King. Seven issues were
defined, as follows:

1. Has violence ceased to be an effective means of ordering
   human life?
2. Should political action have a moral or theological basis?
3. Can active civil disobedience be practiced by large numbers of ordinary people in such a way that social conflicts are nonviolently resolved?
4. Will America in the 1970s be sufficiently different from
   South Africa and India in Gandhi's time to warrant a rejection of Gandhi's teaching by dissatisfied people or a
   suppression of Gandhian tactics if they are employed by
   any considerable segment of the population?
5. In the education of children should we stress technical
   competence or character development?
6. Are such controversies as Nonviolence vs. Black Power,
   Pacifism vs. National Security, Segregation vs. Integration and Morality vs. Due Process debatable?
7. Is there something wrong with our statement of the issues?

The document was sent to several hundred members of the
Southern Illinois University faculty, a rather large number of
graduate students, and nearly a hundred professors at other
universities. The document called attention to American efforts to control violence and American forms of civil disobedience. These American ideas ranged from moralistic and
transcendental beliefs, that had some similarity to Gandhi's
teachings, to secular movements that had almost none of
Gandhi's orientation. The document correctly noted that
Gandhi was widely misinterpreted in this country, both by his
admirers and by his detractors, because "nonviolence" and
"conscientious disobedience" were not unfamiliar terms and
Americans had, in many cases, jumped to the conclusion that

Gandhi was advocating exactly what they were familiar with.

A number of the professors and students, who commented on the document, made interesting points concerning the differences, for example, between Gandhi and Thoreau, and the differences between the problems and resources available to Gandhi and those available to Americans who undertook to use Gandhi's philosophy and tactics. These responses encouraged the Committee to believe that they had hit upon a fecund approach to the question: How much relevance does Gandhi's example and teaching have to contemporary America?

On the other hand, there were reasons for mistrusting the document and some of the comments. In the first place, some of the knowledgeable people to whom we sent the document said nothing except the usual polite thing: "It's an interesting statement," etc. What was more disturbing, there were some old hands, who said, in effect, "When you separate these various doctrines and issues, you miss a certain wholeness or unity that characterized Gandhi's career." They also complained that the alternatives were not adequately stated. At this point we felt like Daniel Boone in the wilderness, not lost, but "bewildered for several days."

Reflecting upon these symptoms of futility, however, we thought we saw the trouble. We had juxtaposed Gandhi's teachings and American ideas without specifying a point of view. We had asked whether violence was an obsolete means of ordering human life, as if such a question could be completely general, with the presumption that a public official, an agitator with a grievance, a citizen who mainly wanted not to be disturbed, and a research professor publishing a study, could all ask the same question and arrive at one plausible answer.

This posing of general questions fills many books and journals and, no doubt, it has its uses. But, for a study of Gandhi, it is inappropriate. Gandhi was a man of action. He often said that there was no science of nonviolence (*ahimsa*). Although his speeches and editorials will fill many volumes—he engaged waff _

in propaganda for over fifty years—they do not constitute a "system." And foreigners who react to Gandhi do not meet him on his own terms, if they pretend to speak and think from an Olympian point of view.

In order to determine whether one is or is not a Gandhian, one must identify the conflicts in which one is involved and the sort of activities that one is carrying on. Because we are university people, the questions that are meaningful and alive for us (with reference to Gandhi) are questions about what we might be doing. We shall, therefore, review Gandhi's words and deeds selectively, paying attention particularly to whatever seems relevant to such questions as these:

How are teachers and students related to the massive social conflicts of our time?

Can we honestly hope for a way out of the impasses in these turbulent confrontations?

What kind of learning do we regard as of most worth, and are we doing all that can be done to provide opportunities for such learning?

In our interpretations of Gandhi we have received much help from five Indian scholars who were visitors on our campus: Dr. Humayan Kabir, Professor A. K. DasGupta, Vice-Chancellor Kalu Lal Shrimali, Professor Antsher Lobo, and Professor N. A. Nikam. For a careful criticism of certain portions of the book we are indebted to the following colleagues: Professors Henry Dan Piper, Paul Arthur Schilpp, Don Ihde, and S. Kumar Jain. For typing the manuscript we wish to thank Mrs. Margaret Plucinsky. And, for suggestions and aids, too numerous to mention, we thank Dean Clarence Hendershot, Mr. C. Kumararatrum, and other members of the Gandhi Centennial Committee. We also are indebted to more than thirty of our colleagues whose publications threw light on many dark places in our wanderings. Finally, the Committee could not have carried out such an ambitious celebration of Gandhi's Centennial, if President Delyte W. Morris had not found the necessary funds and, through the years, led the University toward a full awareness of its international responsibilities.

Contents

ONE

Gandhi's Example

1

Gandhi's "Future" and Ours

How CAN a study of Gandhi's career possibly help American teachers and students to think about the future, *their* future? Of all the topics on which Gandhi spoke and editorialized, "the future" and "education" evoked the strangest comments. Not a few admirers, who often quote what he said about "non-violence" and "justice," seldom mention what he said about the proper subjects for study and the village life for which he wanted to prepare the young.

The "future," for which Gandhi worked was to be pre-dominantly an agrarian society of small, almost self-sufficient, villages. And in this future society, he hoped that the universities would transfer to other agencies the technological services which they had been performing for government and industry.

Could any set of opinions be farther from reasonable expectations? Was Gandhi not, in these respects, a reactionary, looking backward instead of forward?

In proposing serious reflection upon teachings that have been distasteful to some of Gandhi's most loyal followers, we are not assuming that the *Mahatma* had any supernatural gift of prophecy. Quite possibly, the world of the future will bear little resemblance to his vision and, the odds are, the universities will never follow his recommendations.

We do, however, credit Gandhi with an uncanny ability to touch raw nerves, to disturb respectable complacencies, and to open up new lines of thought and action. He shook up many well-informed men who thought they had sound opinions about international trade, about the colonial system, about racial and religious discrimination, and about the proper use of force. His gadfly services on those subjects are comparable to the disturbing challenges of Socrates, of Diogenes and St. Francis. Is it possible that most of us need to be shaken out of our orthodoxies concerning the future industrialization of the world and the place of the universities in that future?

In one sense, it is absurd to ask "What will the future be like?" The future in which we are interested is the future of complex institutions and our roles in them. We would like to forecast, not something that will happen under carefully controlled laboratory conditions, but events that are affected by unnumbered contingencies. Yet, however ignorant we are, we act; and acting, we make assumptions about the future. As De Jouvenel has said, conjecturing about the future would be absurd, if it were avoidable.[1] As long as we are going to act upon the basis of conjectures, we might as well do what we can to improve our forecasts.

In the many recent attempts to predict major social trends for the next generation, the most common assumption is that industrialization will continue to change the face of the globe and the ways of life for more and more human beings. Quite possibly, this expectation will prove to be correct. But are there blind spots in our vision, blind spots to which a dead saint can call our attention?

The current studies of the future try to avoid the too-simple techniques of yesterday's false prophets. They extrapolate statistical curves, but they look for circumstances that might prevent the prolongation of a recent trend. They are not above using an analogy or a model, but they usually examine several of them. They project the repercussions of alternative events.[2]

It is obvious that most of the popular prognostications are guarded by gloomy footnotes that worry over the possibility of nuclear war. And the fragmenting of former empires into mini-states runs counter to what economic planners here and in the

Marxist countries regard as long-term developments. Even in the university cloisters there are bearded young instructors and unconventional students who are out of step with the local marching band: they seem to be marching to the tattoo of some distant, otherworldly drummer.

The study of the future is, in part, an exploration of ourselves. It brings to the surface the hidden corners of our own value systems. If we can be said to have a value system, it is the melange of preferences, fears and aspirations that may be called forth by the events in which we are involved. Parts of our value system are hidden, because there is nothing in our present experience to evoke them. The contemplation of unrealized possibilities in the world of the future does trigger these latent attitudes.

Here is the reason why Gandhi may help us in our study of the future. The future which he envisaged and for which he worked is different from the future contemplated by most of us. He knew as much as we do about the nineteenth-century industrial revolution, but he did not agree with the Spencerians and Marxists who expected mechanization and large-scale organization to be the wave of the future.

Gandhi was very much aware of the intensification of social conflict. Like everyone else in his time, he knew that hitherto submerged and silent classes were stirring. But he accepted as certain neither a final Armageddon nor a miraculous harmonization of contending claims.

Gandhi also thought about the rise of empires and the growing power of states. Projecting from these facts Tennyson had foreseen the parliament of man, a world order guided by great statesmen; while the Comtes and the Mills expected the sciences to enlighten the future rulers of humanity. Gandhi saw the vast imperial regimes as structures built on sand and their officials, misguided by unnecessarily complicated sociology, as lacking in an elemental moral insight.

Anticipations and plans may all be, to some extent, wishful. If so, we propose to be guided for a while by Gandhi's wishes. Reacting to the future for which he hoped, we may escape—

for a time—the passions that control our own thoughts.
The "we" in this book, when it is not an editorial "we,"
refers to university people, sometimes the academicians at our
own university and sometimes to the teachers, officers and students of American universities generally. This "we" will probably exceed our powers of generalization, but it should make
the reported and asserted reactions to Gandhi's "future" more
reliable than if we claimed to speak for the whole citizenry of
our land.

2

Gandhi on Nonviolent Civil Disobedience

IN AN age troubled by wars and civil commotion, Gandhi became the symbol and the spokesman for nonviolence. Friend and foe, alike, were impressed by what he was able to accomplish without resort to armed force. He mobilized and unified thousands of poor, isolated, and largely illiterate villages in the pursuit of their rights and of nationhood. In the face of hateful provocations and endless frustrations, Gandhi created a discipline that brought a great empire to terms. Of course, there were failures along the way. And, at the end of his life, Gandhi failed to achieve a nonviolent rapprochement between Hindus and Moslems. But his bloodless victories were so spectacular that even the most cynical observers could not dismiss nonviolence as a visionary pipedream.

Today, a century after Gandhi's birth and two decades after his death, conflict seems to be unavoidable. It is now potentially more destructive than ever. Can the issues that divide nations, races, and classes be resolved in Gandhi's way? And, regardless of the chances of success, will nonviolence command the respect of good men?

If Gandhian nonviolence cannot be ignored, what burdens does it lay upon teachers and students? Does it challenge the ways in which schools are now related to social conflicts? To answer these questions, we propose to examine Gandhi's teaching and his practice. The orientation of American educational institutions is in a tradition that contrasts in many ways with the tradition from which Gandhi sprang.

Religious Background

Gandhi's conception of nonviolence was rooted in the complex Indian religions. That will be the first point to be understood. At the same time, traditional doctrines were given a revolutionary interpretation. Some appreciation, both of the tradition and of Gandhi's innovations, is required in order to make sense of his peculiar combinations of suffering and activism, of respect for law and disobedience.

The "religion," on which Gandhi based his political practices, was neither formal nor institutional. Rather, it was that "which binds one indissolubly to the truth within and which ever purifies."[1] But, what is Truth? Gandhi replies that it is "a difficult question; but I have solved it for myself by saying that it is what the voice within tells you."[2] Sometimes, however, Gandhi equates Truth with God, Self-knowledge, and so on. Now, "devotion to this Truth is the sole justification for our existence. All our activities should be centered in Truth. Truth should be the very breath of our life. When once this stage in the pilgrim's progress is reached, all other rules of correct living will come without effort, and obedience to them will be instinctive. But without Truth, it would be impossible to observe any principles or rules in life."[3] Holding onto Truth is what Gandhi calls *"Satyagraha." "Satyagraha* is literally holding onto Truth and it means, therefore, Truthforce. Truth is soul or spirit. It is, therefore, known as soulforce."[4] Though the justification of our existence lies in our devotion to Truth, "it is impossible for us to realize perfect Truth so long as we are imprisoned in this mortal frame."[5]

The way leading to Truth lies in *ahimsa* or nonviolence. *Ahimsa*, for Gandhi, has positive and negative connotations. In its positive connotation, it means unbounded love, affection, and sympathy; and in its negative aspect, it means noninjury to any living creature, in thought, word, and deed. Therefore, he points out that:

> Without *ahimsa*, it is not possible to seek and find Truth.
> *Ahimsa* and Truth are so intertwined that it is practically
> impossible to disentangle and separate them. They are like
> the two sides of a coin, or rather of a smooth unstamped
> metallic disc. Who can say, which is the obverse, and
> which is the reverse? Nevertheless, *ahimsa* is the means;
> Truth is the end. Means, to be means, must always be
> within our reach, and so *ahimsa* is our supreme duty.[6]

The seeker after Truth, therefore, has to be firmly committed to nonviolence. That commitment to nonviolence is the supreme duty of man is not an original conception, but is, in fact, the expression of a very ancient Indian tradition. *Ahimsa* was recognized as a value in Indian thought as early as the Upanishadic period (700–300 B.C.) when the seers condemned sacrifices which involved violence in order to propitiate the gods. But the conception, of course, became more explicit when Gautama, the Buddha, (around 560–480 B.C.) revolted against all forms of killing and the destruction of innocent animals in Vedic rituals. From this period onwards, *ahimsa*, as a moral value pervades the Indian tradition.

Buddha justifies nonviolence on the ethical plane. According to him, the world is full of suffering, and there are many causes for suffering. Suffering can be prevented by removing those causes. Wanton violence on living beings causes suffering. Buddha, therefore, urged people to be in no way the cause of suffering of other creatures; at the same time they should do their best to remove suffering in the world. *Dhammapada*, the Bible of the Buddhists, therefore, says that without commitment to nonviolence, *nirvana* is impossible for man. The first of the ten precepts that Buddha gave for right behavior enjoins man to refrain from causing the death of living beings.

In terms of actual practice, Jainism, which had an origin

that was contemporaneous with Buddhism, is the most thoroughgoing and rigorous in its interpretation of nonviolence. According to the Jains, directly doing violence, indirectly causing it, and even standing by and permitting violence should be avoided, if the *ahimsa* commandment is to be strictly followed. "The scrupulous enforcement of this rule," Dr. Radhakrishnan points out, "has led to many practices which come in for cheap sneering at the hands of unsympathetic students. Lest any life be destroyed, some Jains sweep the ground as they go, walk veiled for fear of inhaling a living organism, strain water, and reject even honey."[7]

Ahimsa, we have seen, should not be interpreted as a merely negative principle of noninjury or non-killing. It is a positive principle of loving all creatures as well. As a kind of love, it is clear, *ahimsa* represents something that is common to many of the religions in the East and in the West. The Indian conception of *ahimsa* goes beyond the Western conceptions of love in that it does not limit itself to the *human* world, but extends to all living creatures.

"Truth and non-violence are as old as the hills," said Gandhi, and his advocacy of nonviolence, therefore, is not anything new or spectacular. He also agrees with Max Müller's dictum that "truth needed to be repeated, as long as there were men who disbelieved it."[8] What is new and original with Gandhi is not his mere repetition of what passes for truth, but the clarifying of some of the far-reaching implications of the sacred doctrine. These implications are made explicit in his "experiments" with truth.

Gandhi recognizes, in consonance with Indian tradition, that one should not do violence to any living creature and should love the meanest of creatures as oneself. A difficult problem immediately presents itself. Shall we not kill the insects, reptiles, tigers, etc.? Shall we actually show love towards them? Gandhi's reply to this critical question is that, though *ahimsa* is a categorical imperative, it allows exceptions in so far as we are human, and human living always involves some kind of *himsa* or violence. He says:

In life, it is impossible to eschew violence completely. Now the question arises, where is one to draw the line? The line cannot be the same for everyone. For, although, essentially, the principle is the same, yet everyone applies it in his or her own way. What is one man's food can be another's poison. . . .

If I wish to be an agriculturist and stay in a jungle, I will have to use the minimum unavoidable violence, in order to protect my fields. I will have to kill monkeys, birds, and insects, which eat up my crops. If I do not wish to do so myself, I will have to engage someone to do it for me. There is not much difference between the two. To allow crops to be eaten up by animals, in the name of *ahimsa*, while there is a famine in the land, is certainly a sin. Evil and good are relative terms. What is good under certain conditions can become an evil or a sin, under a different set of conditions.

Man is not to drown himself in the well of *shastras* (sacred scriptures), but he is to dive in their broad ocean and bring out pearls. At every step, he has to use his discrimination, as to what is *ahimsa* and what is *himsa*.[9]

Gandhi's Novel Use of the Idea

Gandhi's conception of *ahimsa* is, therefore, not rigid but flexible. Though nonviolence is a prima facie duty, it cannot be applied in a mechanical way to actual duties in life situations. Gandhi's interest was not only in the enunciation of the principle, but also in its application as well. No line, as Gandhi said, can be drawn between violence and nonviolence. As we delve deep into the concept, it becomes more and more elusive.

Elsewhere, he draws the distinction between violence and nonviolence by pointing out that "the essence of violence is that there must be a violent intention behind a thought, word, or act, i.e., an intention to do harm to the opponent so called."[10] But too much should not be made of these distinctions. Gandhi's conception of *ahimsa* is essentially dynamic and "experimental." During the course of some fifty years of experiments, he had to engage in many problems of casuistry. What is important for us it not whether a particular case is an instance of violence or nonviolence, but the radical implications of the principle itself. What are the implications of nonviolence? First of all, Gandhi transformed the notion of nonviolence from an individual pursuit to a collective revolution. "Religion of non-violence," Gandhi said, "is not meant merely for the *rishis* and saints. It is meant for the common people as well."[11]

A reading of Indian history suggests that, in spite of the people's commitment to and faith in nonviolence, its record is a record of wars, many of them defensive wars, but, nonetheless, wars. This state of affairs was rationalized by emphasizing nonviolence at the individual level as a means of salvation (*moksa* or *nirvana*). The paradox was an endorsement of nonviolence at the individual level and an acquiescence in violence at the collective level. Violence and nonviolence thus coexisted until Gandhi's time.

Gandhi was to show the practicability of "the impossible," viz., the practice of nonviolence collectively. This was a new thought for most of the Hindus. It was also a new thought for most of the people of other traditions. Martin Luther King testified to that when he wrote: "Prior to reading Gandhi, I had about concluded that the ethics of Jesus were only effective in individual relationships. The 'turn the other cheek' philosophy and the 'love your enemies' philosophy were only valid, I felt, when individuals were in conflict with other individuals; when racial groups and nations were in conflict, a more realistic approach seemed necessary. But, after reading Gandhi, I saw how utterly mistaken I was."[12]

Gandhi not only saw *ahimsa* as a *collective* practice, he saw that men did not yet *know* all they needed to know about the application of the principle. Love rather than hate is the law of our species; but, more than ever before, what is now required is further exploration in the field of nonviolence. "We are constantly being astonished these days at the amazing discoveries in the field of violence. But I maintain that far more undreamt of and seemingly impossible discoveries will be made

in the field of nonviolence."[13] The fact that violence exists in
the world is not the rule, but the exception, and Gandhi argues
very vehemently to prove that nonviolence is the law of the
world:

> I claim that even now, though the social structure is not
> based on a conscious acceptance of non-violence, all the
> world over mankind lives and men retain their possessions
> on the sufferance of one another. If they had not done so,
> only the fewest and the most ferocious would have survived.
> But such is not the case. Families are bound together by
> ties of love, and so are groups in the so-called civilized
> society called nations. Only they do not recognize the
> supremacy of the law of non-violence. . . . The many
> failures we see are not of the law but of the followers,
> many of whom do not even know that they are under that
> law willy-nilly. When a mother dies for her child, she
> unknowingly obeys the law. I have been pleading for the
> past fifty years for a conscious acceptance of the law and
> its zealous practice, even in the face of failures. Fifty years'
> work has shown marvellous results and strengthened my
> faith.[14]

Nonviolence is not only the law of the human species, but is,
in fact, the principle which governs the cosmos. "I have found,"
Gandhi said, "that life persists in the midst of destruction and,
therefore, there must be a higher law than that of destruction.
Only under that law would a well-ordered society be intel-
ligible and life worth living."[15]

However necessary *ahimsa* may be, it is a difficult way of
life. Commitment to nonviolence comes only with the elimina-
tion of all ill will. It is the absence of hatred that makes possible the transformation of opponents. The wrongdoer, who
was bowed down through violent means, retaliates as soon as
he finds himself strong again; but the wrongdoer, who is transformed through nonviolence, becomes an asset to the society.
Not by violence, but by nonviolence, can a society be transformed.

To transform an individual or society through nonviolent

means involves personal suffering of the devotees of *ahimsa*. It is not by inflicting violence, but by suffering it, that the transformation of the wicked and unjust individual is possible. "The hardest heart and the grossest ignorance must disappear before the rising sun of suffering without anger and without malice."[16] To suffer injustice may lead to passivity, but Gandhi makes it clear that nonviolence is not passive but active. "No man could be actively non-violent and not rise against social injustice no matter where it occurred."[17] Again, according to Gandhi, "Non-violence is 'not a resignation from all real fighting against wickedness.' On the contrary, the non-violence of my conception is a more active and real fight against wickedness than retaliation whose very nature is to increase wickedness."[18]

In view of the discipline required, Gandhi declares that a perfect practice of nonviolence is possible only for the brave. It is not possible for cowards. It is for the strong, not the weak. "Between violence and cowardly flight," Gandhi said, "I can only prefer violence to cowardice. I can no more preach non-violence to a coward than I can tempt a blind man to enjoy healthy scenes. Non-violence is the summit of bravery. And, in my own experience, I have had no difficulty in demonstrating to men trained in the school of violence the superiority of non-violence. As a coward, which I was for years, I harboured violence. I began to prize non-violence only when I began to shed cowardice."[19]

Finally, nonviolence can never be the product of violence, because violent means can never produce nonviolent ends. The arguments of individuals and nations arming themselves in order to maintain "peace" did not appeal to Gandhi. In order to say that one is nonviolent, it is not necessary that he should first be violent. As an old Indian saying goes, to say that my hands are clean does not mean that I have first put them in the mud and then washed them. "It has been suggested by American friends that the atom bomb will bring in *ahimsa*, as nothing else can. It will, if it is meant that its destructive power will so disgust the world, that it will turn it away from violence for the time being. And this is very like a man glutting himself with the dainties to the point of nausea, and turning away from them only to return with redoubled zeal after the effect of nausea is well over. Precisely in the same manner will the world return to violence with renewed zeal, after the effect of disgust is worn out."[20]

An unwary reader might complain that there is something mystical in the entire notion of *Satyagraha* and the language of truth and nonviolence in which Gandhi speaks. We have considered certain implications of non-violence. But what does it mean to say that we should hold on to Truth? The notion of *Satyagraha*, however, is not as mysterious as Gandhi's language sometimes suggests. Gandhi, the man of action, is sometimes more easily understood than the words in which he formulates his doctrines. Gandhi's own application of *Satyagraha* points to two related things. Negatively, it enjoins upon man the duty to eradicate evil, and positively, it reminds him to follow his conscience and serve the community. Thus, throughout his life, Gandhi was striving to root out evil practices and age-old prejudices, such as the inequality of men, racial and communal hatred, the practice of untouchability in India, and so on. Positively, his constructive program includes experiments in "basic education," promotion of *khadi* (hand-spun cloth) and village industries, inculcating a sense of self-respect in the oppressed and downtrodden people, and so on. This service to the community in its perfect form is possible only when one identifies himself with the joys and sorrows of the world, without denying the duty to follow conscience. "Whenever I see an erring man," said Gandhi, "I say to myself I have also erred; when I see a lustful man I say to myself, so was I once; and in this way I feel kinship with everyone in the world and feel that I cannot be happy without the humblest of us being happy."[21] Shorn of all the mystical vocabulary, *Satyagraha* may be viewed 1) as a way of life exemplified in Gandhi himself, and 2) as a technique of domestic, social, and political action with a view to bringing about desired change, through peaceful and nonviolent means, for the common good. *Satyagraha* is resistance to injustice on the one hand, and following one's conscience and promoting the common good in a peaceful and constructive way, on the other.

Since the aims of education, according to Gandhi, are the pursuit of truth and the promotion of common good, his statement that *Satyagraha* should be an integral part of education is not surprising. In fact, Gandhi goes further than this and says that "*Satyagraha* is the noblest and best education. It should come, not after the ordinary education in letters, of children, but it should precede it. It will not be denied, that a child, before it begins to write its alphabet and to gain wordly knowledge, should know what the soul is, what truth is, what love is, what powers are latent in the soul. It should be an essential of real education that a child should learn, that in the struggle of life, it can easily conquer hate by love, untruth by truth, violence by self-suffering."[22]

What is interesting about *Satyagraha* is that it does not remain a metaphysical concept shining in its own glory. It is rather a principle which is manifested in every field of human activity. "In referring to the universality of *Satyagraha*, I have time and again observed in these columns that it is capable of application in the social no less than in the political field. It may equally be employed against Government, society, or one's own family, father, mother, husband, or wife, as the case may be. For, it is the beauty of this spiritual weapon that when it is completely free from the taint of *himsa* and its use is actuated purely and solely by love it may be used with absolute impunity in any connection and in any circumstances whatever."[23] *Satyagraha*, as applied to the social structure of the community, essentially consists in nonconformity with evil customs and practices, and as applied in the political structure, it is known as civil disobedience.

Relation of Civil Disobedience to Ahimsa

Since Gandhi's statements on the problem of civil disobedience are numerous and repeatedly explained, we can be sure of his position in great detail. Civil disobedience is not offered as a technique only, and it is not appropriate merely in political institutions. Nonconformist attitudes are appropriate at times in all social institutions. Take, for example, strikes and boycotts in educational institutions. Gandhi points out that, unlike strikes in industrial establishments, strikes in educational institutions must be rare. "Unlike labourers, students are educated and can have no material interest to serve by means of strikes, and unlike employers, heads of educational institutions have no interest in conflict with that of the students."[24] While occasions for strikes in schools must, therefore, be rare, "it is not impossible to conceive such as to warrant strikes on their part. Thus, for instance, if a principal running counter to public opinion refuses to recognize a day of universal rejoicing as a holiday which both parents and their school- or college-going children may desire, students will be justified in declaring a strike for that day."[25]

It is possible that Gandhi would have recognized more occasions for school strikes, if he had been more familiar with the internal conflicts of contemporary educational systems. In any case, he refers to the schools when he wishes to stress, not only the applicability of civil disobedience to all human affairs, but also the need for adapting the idea to the peculiar conflicts of each institution.

Every institution, including the political and legal institutions, has certain limited functions to perform. The fact that an individual is a member of an institution does not mean that he is bound to obey all the rules of such an institution, however bad they are. The individual always retains the right to disobey those rules which are evil. Commenting on the interference by educational institutions with the political views of the students, Gandhi says:

> The function of educational institutions is to impart education to the boys and girls who choose to join them and therethrough to help to mould their character, never to interfere with their political or other non-moral activities outside the school room.[26]

The rules that are to be followed, even in school strikes are the same as in major civil disobedience movements. Thus,

Gandhi points out that "If students have a real grievance against their teachers, they may have the right to strike and even picket their school or college, but only to the extent of politely warning the unwary from attending their classes. They could do so by speaking or by distributing leaflets. But they may not obstruct the passage or use any coercion against those who do not want to strike."[27]

After this detour concerning students and their right to disobey the rules of educational institutions, let us now turn to an examination of Gandhi's main views on Civil Disobedience.[28]

Gandhi borrowed the phrase, "civil disobedience," from the famous essay by Henry David Thoreau. The borrowing occurred some years after he had gotten the idea of *Satyagraha*. From time to time, he made various distinctions between the practices that he called civil disobedience and practices that he considered less worthy. Gandhi treats civil disobedience as a species of an essentially spiritual principle, *Satyagraha*, "the exercise of the purest soul force in its perfect form. . . . For this exercise, prolonged training of the individual is an absolute necessity, so that a perfect *Satyagrahi* has to be almost, if not entirely, a perfect man."[29] *Satyagraha*, as applied in the political structure of a community, manifests itself then as civil disobedience, and Gandhi defines civil disobedience as "the civil breach of unmoral statutory enactments."[30] In contrast to the Thomistic tradition, which contends that an unjust law is no law at all, and the recent American practice, which makes disobedience a means of "law-testing," Gandhi does not seem to doubt the legal status of the disputed orders, but only their justness or morality.

Civil Disobedience is essentially a dynamic concept and involves active resistance to unjust laws. It is not passive resistance.

Passive Resistance is used in the orthodox English sense and covers the suffragette movement as well as the resistance of the non-conformists. Passive resistance has been conceived and is regarded as a weapon of the weak. Whilst it avoids violence, being not open to the weak, it does not exclude its use if, in the opinion of the passive resister, the occasion demands it.[31]

Civil disobedience, although dynamic, must be, by definition, nonviolent. It is "civil" in the sense that it is not "criminal." And, being civil, no action is attempted and no move is made in secrecy. Just as a criminal is one who is not in the habit of obeying laws, a civil resister is one who is generally a law-abiding citizen. In order, therefore, to undertake civil disobedience, one should have qualified himself as a law-abiding citizen. Moreover, "disobedience to be civil must be sincere, respectful, restrained, never defiant, must be based upon some well-understood principle, must not be capricious, and, above all, must have no ill will or hatred behind it."[32] Civil disobedience may be undertaken either individually or collectively. Since there is always the possibility of a mass civil disobedience becoming violent, Gandhi sometimes advocates that it should be restricted to the *Satyagrahis* who are well-disciplined morally and spiritually. Sometimes, however, Gandhi admits the desirability of mass civil disobedience, assuming that the people are guided by suitable leaders.

Noncooperation

While Gandhi does not, in general, seem to favor mass civil disobedience (unless the people are firmly committed to nonviolence and are pledged to accept suffering), he regards as feasible mass "noncooperation." Noncooperation means withdrawing cooperation from a state that in the noncooperator's view has become corrupt. Noncooperation excludes what Gandhi calls "the fierce type of Civil Disobedience." "By its very nature," he writes, "non-cooperation is even open to children of understanding and can be safely practised by the masses."[33] Whereas civil disobedience involves the active breaking of laws, noncooperation need not do so. There was no law which demanded buying of foreign goods, and the people of India were breaching no law when they boycotted British goods during their Independence movement. Other instances of noncooperation as practised in India were the surrendering of titles, honors, etc., conferred by government, boycotting administrative offices, judicial courts, schools, etc.; resigning from police, military, and other administrative and executive positions; *hartal*, i.e., closing of shops and other business establishments; picketing, and so on.

The effectiveness of noncooperation comes from the dependence of any government, however tyrannical, on the consent of the governed. Large-scale noncooperation can paralyze the regime and bring down the government through peaceful means. Gandhi believed, nevertheless, that a constructive program also has to be formulated for any noncooperation movement if it is to be successful.

Although Gandhi tried to avoid certain difficulties with his distinction between civil disobedience and noncooperation, the distinction tends to disappear in practice, for most noncooperation movements sooner or later violate some law. This is sure to happen if the authorities ban organized picketing or if a boycott is declared to be a conspiracy. Gandhi, therefore, says on another occasion:

> A little reflection will show that civil disobedience is a necessary part of non-cooperation. You assist an administration most effectively by obeying its orders and decrees. An evil administration never deserves such allegiance. Allegiance to it means partaking of the evil. A good man will, therefore, resist an evil system or administration with his whole soul. Disobedience of the laws of an evil State is, therefore, a duty.[34]

Civil disobedience and noncooperation being offshoots of the genre, *Satyagraha*, some of the conditions that Gandhi prescribes for *Satyagraha*, like strict adherence to nonviolence, respect for the opponent, and so on, are applicable to noncooperation as well as to civil disobedience. Gandhi himself does not use these terms consistently, and it is not always easy to say whether a particular action has been performed in the spirit of civil disobedience, passive resistance, noncooperation, or *Satyagraha*.

Gandhi's distinction does not lie just in the enunciation of the familiar doctrine that evil and unjust laws ought to be disobeyed. As in the case of nonviolence, what is distinctive in his thinking is the revolutionary conclusions that he draws from the doctrine. We have seen that the proposition that man should pursue and realize Truth is a categorical imperative for Gandhi. From this it follows that anything which is an impediment to the pursuit of Truth should be overcome. Evil is an impediment to Truth. Therefore, evil should be overcome. The overcoming of evil may be by the infliction of suffering on others, but this increases evil and does not decrease it. Therefore, the infliction of suffering must be on oneself, and Gandhi is emphatic in asserting that the pursuit of Truth necessarily involves suffering on the part of the pursuer. "*Satyagraha* means readiness to suffer and a faith that the more innocent and pure the suffering, the more potent will it be in its effect."[35]

Unjust laws being necessarily evil, a seeker after Truth has the *duty* to resist unjust laws. Gandhi does not speak of civil disobedience as merely the *right* of a citizen, but also as his *duty*. Thus he says: "I wish I could persuade everybody that civil disobedience is the inherent right of a citizen. He dare not give it up without ceasing to be a man."[36] And he goes on to say: "Civil disobedience, therefore, becomes a sacred duty when the State has become lawless, or which is the same thing, corrupt. And a citizen that barters with such a State shares its corruption or lawlessness."[37] When Gandhi uses such phrases as "inherent right" and "birthright" of civil disobedience, he seems to mean something like "natural rights" in Western political theory. But when he speaks about the "duty" of civil disobedience, he means it as a "moral duty." Here, again, is an instance of the intersection of politics and morality in Gandhi's thought.

One has a *duty* to resist an unjust law, because it is a hindrance to the pursuit of Truth, not only for the individual, but also for the legislator or oppressor. Resistance to an unjust law is a self-regarding moral duty, but it is also an other-regarding moral duty. The consequence of this line of reasoning is that one disobeys an unjust law out of a reverence for the moral personality of the opponent. The law which is unjust is an evil, but the *person* who enacted the law is inherently good. "Man and his deed are two distinct things. It is quite proper to resist and attack a system, but to resist and attack its author is tantamount to resisting and attacking oneself."[38] Gandhi also frequently speaks of the "trust" a civil resister should place in the oppressor's potential goodness, the "conversion" of the wrong-doer, and the "weaning away" of one's opponent from error.

Conciliation and Compromise

The fact that Gandhi uses such words as "conversion" and "weaning away" should not lead us to infer that he takes for granted the self-righteousness of the civil resister and the wickedness of the opponent. He frequently argues that a civil resister should view the disputed subject objectively with a detached mind, and that he should give the fullest consideration to all the points of view. "Three-fourths of the miseries and misunderstandings in the world will disappear, if we step into the shoes of our adversaries and understand their standpoint. We will then agree with our adversaries quickly or think of them charitably."[39] Moreover, Gandhi recognizes that though Truth itself is absolute, our notions of truth are sometimes relative and, therefore, there should be room for discussion, negotiation, and reconciliation in our dealings with our opponent. Thus he says: "All my life through, the very insistence on truth has taught me to appreciate the beauty of compromise. I saw later in life that this spirit was an essential part of *Satyagraha*."[40]

Compromise should be based on give-and-take, but there should be no compromise on fundamental principles. What, moveover, is implied in the admission of fallibility is the willingness of the *Satyagrahi* to suffer.

> Q. (Sir Chimanlal): However honestly a man may strive in his search for truth, his notions of truth may be different from the notions of others. Who, then, is to determine the truth?
> A. (M. K. Gandhi): The individual himself would determine that.
> Q. Different individuals would have different views as to truth. Would that not lead to confusion?
> A. I do not think so.
> Q. Honestly striving after truth is different in every case.
> A. That is why the non-violence part was a necessary corollary. Without that there would be confusion and worse.[41]

Therefore, whatever may be the form of *Satyagraha* that one undertakes, nonviolence is a *sine qua non*. Violent civil resistance cannot be justified because it is not morally superior to the position of the state which seeks to maintain its laws forcibly.

The Avoidance of Anarchy and Abuses

The fact that a civil resister who breaks a law is willing cheerfully to undergo punishment does not weaken the political structure of the community, but will, in fact, strengthen it. "Civil disobedience is never followed by anarchy. Criminal disobedience can lead to it. Every state puts down criminal disobedience by force. It perishes, if it does not. But to put down civil disobedience is to attempt to imprison conscience. Civil disobedience can only lead to strength and purity."[42] Again, Gandhi points out that "the real meaning of the statement that we are a law-abiding nation is that we are passive resisters."[43] Showing that he had understood English law, Gandhi remarked that the law does not say "You must do such a thing"; it says "If you do not do it, we will punish you."[44] To disobey a law and suffer the penalty attached to the violation is perfectly legal and, therefore, we may say that a civil resister obeys the law by disobeying it!

Gandhi insists that *Satyagraha* should never be undertaken for purely selfish ends and personal gain; otherwise, "there would be no end of scoundrels blackmailing people by resorting to the means."[45] Nor should it be undertaken out of utilitarian considerations. "A votary of *ahimsa* cannot subscribe to the utilitarian formula (of the greatest good of the greatest number). He will strive for the greatest good of all and die in the attempt to realize the ideal. . . . The utilitarian, to be logical, will never sacrifice himself. The absolutist will even sacrifice himself."[46]

Nor should there be any "game" of *Satyagraha*, using it as an expedient and hitting the opponent when one finds him weak. On this account, Gandhi was often criticized that he did not play *Realpolitik*. The result, his critics contended, was a record of "missed opportunities."[47] For example, when the British strength was deployed and dissipated during World War II, Gandhi could have intensified his *Satyagraha* campaigns in India, making the British stay impossible. But he refused to do so, saying: "It is absurd to launch civil disobedience today for independence. How are we to fight for independence with those whose own independence is in grave peril? Even if independence can be given by one nation to another, it is not possible for the English. Those who are themselves in peril cannot save others. But if they fight unto death for their freedom and they are at all reasonable, they must recognize our right of free speech."[48] Gandhi's career is moulded by many such instances and, as Arne Naess points out, "by not exploiting their advantageous position, Gandhi's supporters remained true to his and their own aim, which was future cooperation with those who were then their opponents."[49]

Because of Gandhi's reputation as a shrewd bargainer and game player, his denials that *Satyagraha* is a game have often fallen on deaf ears. Some of the participants in civil disobedience campaigns have obviously looked upon their own actions, as they are usually viewed by officials, as a kind of bargaining tactics being selected because of their *nuisance value*. This misinterpretation is widespread in the United States, where the nullification tradition is strong and the dominant conception of politics is the idea of agreement on *quid pro quo*.

Nonviolent civil disobedience, as prescribed by Gandhi, is thus much more than a simple stubbornness. It is a strenuous discipline, requiring insight as well as commitment, sensitivity to values as well as indifference to one's own suffering. *Satyagraha* is an achievement; it is not a miraculous gift. It is achieved by deeply religious men who do not run away from human society. The *Satyagrahi* is not dependent upon an existing society for his ideals; yet, his immediate objectives are determined by an imaginative study of the society in which he happens to dwell.

3

Gandhi and the Problem
of Leadership

To WESTERN ears Gandhi's call for courageous action sounds
like a call to leadership. When he asserts that nonviolence is
for the strong and not for the weak, when he makes "impossible" demands for stoical endurance, Gandhi sounds like a
man addressing himself to a few trusted lieutenants who are
capable of initiative. He does not sound like someone who is
broadcasting an appeal to the masses.

Yet, Gandhi did not have two messages, one of them esoteric
and the other, popular. Although he recognized the unread-
iness of the average person for anything beyond passive resistance, he never offered an easy path to the average man. His
speeches in mass meetings set forth a discipline that seems to
Westerners to be appropriate for leaders rather than for followers. But Gandhi said the same thing to followers that he
said to leaders. Indeed, he scarcely had a theory of leadership.

Furthermore, when Gandhi made autobiographical references to himself, there was no suggestion that he was himself
peculiarly fitted for leadership. As he described his discovery
of *Satyagraha*, the insight could not be attributed to native wit
or to unusual schooling. He takes credit for no remarkable
traits of character and he gives very little credit to his teachers.
To paraphrase Shakespeare, he wants us to believe that greatness was thrust upon him.

Few people who knew anything of Gandhi's childhood could have imagined that he would be the unchallenged leader of the four hundred million people of India. Although it is true that there is something unpredictable, call it destiny or chance, that contributes to the rise of a leader, it is widely believed that certain traits, such as, intelligence, courage, outgoingness, etc., are essential ingredients. Gandhi, by his own admission, did not manifest these traits during his childhood. Intellectually, he was average. Nor did he care for academic excellence. "My mind is narrow," says Gandhi. "I have not read much literature. I have not seen much of the world. I have concentrated upon certain things in life and beyond that I have no other interest."[1] Furthermore, he was a "coward" in his childhood. "I used to be haunted by the fear of thieves, ghosts, and serpents. I did not dare to stir out of doors at night. Darkness was a terror to me."[2]

When Gandhi went to England in 1888 to study law, he was hardly eighteen years old. Like any ordinary law student, his ambition then was to make a "good living" out of the legal profession. During the three years of his stay in England, he hardly took any interest in politics or world affairs. Instead, he started a vegetarian club in his locality! "I was elected to the Executive Committee of the Vegetarian Society, and made it a point to attend every one of its meetings, but I always felt tongue-tied. . . . Not that I never felt tempted to speak. But I was at a loss to know how to express myself."[3]

By contrast, Jawaharlal Nehru, who went to study in England in 1905 at the age of sixteen, tells in his *Autobiography* of a very different arrival in England (in 1905):

> I was greatly interested in the General Election, which took place, as far as I remember, at the end of 1905 and which ended in a great Liberal victory. Early in 1906 our form master asked us about the new Government, and, much to his surprise, I was the only boy in his form who could give him much information on the subject. Apart from politics another subject that fascinated

me was the early growth of aviation. Those were the days of the Wright Brothers and Santos-Dumont (to be followed soon by Farnan, Latham, and Bleriot).[4]

Gandhi's interest in political affairs did not come till later in life. World politics did not interest him except in a very indirect way. Gandhi returned to India in 1891 at the age of twenty-two and enrolled as a barrister in the Bombay High Court; but he proved to be a complete failure. The first lawsuit he handled as an attorney was vividly described by him as follows:

> I appeared for the defendant and had thus to cross-examine the plaintiff's witnesses. I stood up, but my heart sank into my boots. My head was reeling and I felt as though the whole court was doing likewise. I could think of no question to ask. The judge must have laughed, and the vakils no doubt enjoyed the spectacle. But I was past seeing anything. I sat down and told the agent that I could not conduct the case, that he had better engage Patel and have the fee back from me. Mr. Patel was duly engaged for Rs. 51. To him, of course, the case was child's play.[5]

Frustrated and disheartened, Gandhi returned to Rajkot, his native place, where, as luck would have it, he got an offer to act as a legal aide to an Indian firm in South Africa. "This was hardly going there as a barrister. It was going as a servant of the firm."[6]

The Turning Point

And so Gandhi sailed to Durban, South Africa, in 1893. It was in this country that the first petals of leadership began to blossom. On the seventh or the eighth day after he arrived in Durban, Gandhi was to go to Pretoria on his company's work. He reserved a first class seat on the train. But as he reached Maritzburg, the capital of Natal, he was asked to vacate his seat and go to the "van compartment" because he was a "colored" man. This Gandhi refused to do. A constable pushed him out of the train, and the train steamed away without him. It was a strange new place and the night was bitterly cold. Gandhi recounts that this incident of personal insult and humiliation was a turning point in his life. The cold shivering night he spent at Maritzburg was a most creative time for him.

> Now the creative experience comes there. I was afraid
> for my very life. I entered the dark waiting room. There
> was a white man in the room. I was afraid of him. What
> is my duty? I asked myself. Should I go back to India,
> or should I go forward, with God as my helper, and face
> whatever was in store for me? I decided to stay and suffer.
> My active non-violence began from that date. And God
> put me through the test during that journey. I was severely
> assaulted by the coach attendant for my moving from the
> seat he had given me. That was one of the richest experi-
> ences of my life.[7]

Although some of the traits that psychologists and soci-ologists commonly attribute to leadership were lacking in Gandhi in his youth, he did possess an abundance of char-acter. "I very jealously guarded my character," says Gandhi. "The least little blemish drew tears from my eyes. When I merited, or seemed to the teacher to merit, a rebuke, it was unbearable for me. I remember having once received corporal punishment. I did not so much mind the punishment, as the fact that it was considered my desert. I wept piteously."[8]

Character is ordinarily manifest in the ability to commit one-self to certain moral rules or principles; in a broader sense, it is a consistent pattern of conduct and behavior. By itself, char-acter may not add greatly to one's leadership qualities, but the lack of it will certainly affect prospects for leadership. A per-son whose actions are inconsistent with what he says is likely to be judged "unreliable" and rejected by potential followers. A group looks to the leader, not only expecting him to practice what he preaches, but also expecting him to exemplify a certain minimum morality.

Identification with the Common People

Strength of character, a peculiarly individual trait, may be *necessary* to leadership, but it is not a *sufficient* qualification. A leader must, in addition, maintain communication between himself and the people whom he leads. By "communication" we mean not just intellectual discourse, but an active sharing, participation and identification. It is in his identification with the masses,—identification with their way of life, their hopes and aspirations,—that Gandhi's leadership qualities emerge. Whereas Gandhi's strength of character made him a great man, his identification with the masses made him a great leader. Identification does not mean "representation" of the people, as representation is understood in Western countries. Gandhi is, as Jawaharlal Nehru puts it, "the quintessence of the conscious and subconscious will of those millions. It is perhaps something more than representation; for he is the idealized personification of those vast millions."[9]

A man who identifies himself completely with a people might, of course, become one among them and not a leader at all. He should, in addition, also transcend them, sometimes disregarding what they stand for. Gandhi was emphatic about this.

> Those who claim to lead the masses must resolutely refuse to be led by them, if we want to avoid mob law and desire ordered progress for the country. I believe that mere protestation of one's opinion and surrender to the mass opinion is not only not enough, but in matters of vital importance, leaders must *act* contrary to the mass of opinion if it does not commend itself to their reason.[10]

When Gandhi wore the loincloth, lived in mud houses, survived on peanuts and goat's milk, and traveled on foot, bullock-carts and third-class railway carriages, he identified himself with what the Indians call the *daridra-narayana*, the poorest and the lowliest. But Gandhi did more than renounce material goods and comforts. What he did was to awaken the masses from their age-old lethargy and slumber and show them a new world of hope and a future. The "new world" that Gandhi promised was, in fact, old, but it was new in the sense that it did not include a lot of rubbish that had come to be associated with the "tradition." The promise of a brand new world might have overawed the masses for a while, but sooner or later its newness would have aroused suspicions. The promise of the old world without its known blemishes made the people place their confidence in what Gandhi said.

In the context of Indian society, where great masses were ignorant and illiterate, it was no easy task even to *show* them the hope of a better world. Gandhi, for this purpose, spoke to the masses in their own language. Typically, the other Indian leaders of the period were "a queer mixture of East and West, out of place everywhere, at home nowhere." Gandhi was deeply rooted in the tradition, and spoke the language of the tradition. "Just as David, when they put Saul's armor on him, laid it aside and took the pebbles from his own brook, so the Mahatma laid aside the social armor of the West and took the simple pebbles out of his own national brook."[11]

Gandhi adopted certain traditional notions like *Satya* (Truth), *Ahimsa* (nonviolence), and *Tapas* (suffering), notions which are deeply ingrained in the religion and culture of the Indian people, and gave them new meanings. Thus, for example, a saint in Indian tradition, is *popularly* known as a recluse. Gandhi showed by precept and example that one need not retire from the world in his search for Truth. Likewise, there is nothing in Indian tradition which associates the seeking of truth with the breaking of unjust laws, but Gandhi somehow "found" his revolutionary idea in ancient lore. Gandhi's reading of the *Bhagavad-Gita* (part of the Bible of the Hindus) as advocating a philosophy of nonviolence is, again, a strained interpretation which is not shared by most Indian scholars. So is his coining of the expression *Rama-Rajya* to describe an ideal India: this phrase brought up the memory of the great mythological king of Ayodhya, Rama, and the perfection he established on earth during his reign.

The Moral Appeal

Scholars might dispute Gandhi's interpretation of the Indian tradition, and philosophers might argue about his all-too-simple metaphysics. But it should be remembered that Gandhi's use of tradition and metaphysics was *not* intended as an appeal to the scholars; nor were these doctrines intended as a tricky appeal to the feelings and prejudices of the masses. Gandhi's appeal was essentially to character and respect for discipline, and in this appeal he was amazingly successful. History records few instances of leaders holding together a numerous people by appealing to their strength of character. This was possible for Gandhi, because the tradition in which he was grounded was the religious tradition of India, and his communication to the masses was through the language of religion. This was no accident, and it was not hypocrisy. By training and temperament, Gandhi was a religious man. By "religion," of course, he did not mean any formal or institutional religion. What he had in mind was a knowledge of the self and a quest after Truth.

> To see the universal and all-pervading Spirit of Truth face to face one must be able to love the meanest of creation as oneself. And a man who aspires after that cannot afford to keep out of any field of life. That is why my devotion to truth has drawn me into the field of politics; and I can say without the slightest hesitation, and yet in all humility, that those who say that religion has nothing to do with politics do not know what religion means.[12]

And so, his politics being derived from religion, Gandhi became a statesman by becoming a saint.

Indians always idealized the saints; people turned to them for advice and guidance. In a real sense, they were the leaders of the people—leaders, not in the organizational, but in the symbolic sense. Organizational leaders were merely *respected*; they were not revered; they played only a secondary role in

Indian tradition. When sainthood and statesmanship were combined in the same person, the result was the "spiritualizing" of politics and here, in fact, lay Gandhi's strength. In Gandhi's *Satyagraha* campaigns, we find an instance of spiritualization. Keep pure your means and the end takes care of itself, he said. He adopted nonviolence which, for him, was essentially a spiritual principle, as the purest means possible and linked it with the political principle of Indian independence.

However religious the people may be, they know that religion may not by itself "deliver the goods." This handicap of a religious appeal was overcome by the fact that, by the time Gandhi entered the Indian political scene, people were already aware of his successes in South Africa. The practicality of his program had been demonstrated in action. Moreover, Gandhi himself disclaimed being a visionary. He described himself as a "practical idealist." The spiritual, he pointed out, need not be opposed to the practical. "If any action of mine claimed to be spiritual is proved to be unpracticable," Gandhi said, "it must be pronounced to be a failure. I do believe that the most spiritual act is the most practical in the true sense of the term."[13]

Perhaps, the most surprising trait in the Gandhian personality was his sense of humor. Religious piety and a demanding morality are usually associated with grim sobriety and, sometimes, even with sourness. Gandhi, on the contrary, although not a "wit," was frequently in a playful mood. When he encountered peasants and local leaders that he had not seen for some time, he engaged in "small talk," inquiring about their family and personal affairs. Great public issues did not blot out his interest in people as persons. And, as his many photographs prove, his facial expression was frequently a smile, or, even, a grin. What is more amazing is the fact that he could laugh at himself. He occasionally referred to his "crankisms." Gandhi could also laugh in a genial way at his opponents. His autobiographical narratives show that he saw at least some of his adversaries as ridiculous and in need of a little common sense rather than as the embodiment of unadulterated Evil.

These were the lines along which Gandhi's leader-follower relationships developed. Once they were firmly established, Gandhi's followers looked to him for guidance not only in political affairs, but also in spiritual matters. It was now only a short step to a charismatic personality. The people made him a *mahatma* (Great Soul) and not infrequently was he on the threshold of becoming "the Incarnation of God," though Gandhi always denied any such divine mission or supernatural powers.

Political Judgment

The reasons for this charisma, aside from his sensitivity to the concerns of poor and tradition-bound people, may be found in his timely judgments of complicated practical situations. In matters of political action, especially, Gandhi relied on his personal intuitions. Although this fact made the general masses think that Gandhi had some kind of revelation, his more intellectual followers were surprised, baffled and even sometimes angered, because they did not understand what Gandhi was up to. Jawaharlal Nehru thus points out that "his (Gandhi's) way of springing surprises upon us frightened me; there was something unknown about him which, in spite of the closest association for fourteen years, I could not understand at all and which filled me with apprehension. He admitted the presence of this unknown element in him, and said that he himself could not answer for it or foretell what it might lead to."[14] What was "frightening" about such intuitions was his followers' inability to understand the "strategy" behind Gandhi's decisions. Thus, for example, Gandhi called off a nationwide civil resistance movement in 1922 because a small mob in a remote village of Chauri Chaura resorted to violence and attacked a police station. Commenting on this action, Nehru writes:

> The sudden suspension of our movement after the
> Chauri Chaura incident was resented, I think, by almost all
> the prominent Congress leaders—other than Gandhiji,

of course . . . What troubled us even more were the
reasons given for this suspension and the consequences
that seemed to flow from them. Chauri Chaura may
have been and was a deplorable occurrence and wholly
opposed to the spirit of the non-violent movement; but
were a remote village and a mob of excited peasants in
an out-of-the-way place going to put an end, for some
time at least, to our national struggle for freedom? If
this was the inevitable consequence of a sporadic act of
violence, then surely there was something lacking in
the philosophy and technique of a non-violent struggle.[15]

Anyone who attempts to find a "strategy" behind Gandhi's
calling off of the civil resistance movement will be disap-
pointed, because there was no strategy. He felt that such
occurrences as the Chauri Chaura incident would not be in the
spirit of nonviolent resistance. And it is an amazing fact that
Gandhi could cut through and identify a moral issue in what
had appeared to be merely a technical question to most observers. Civil resistance, as we have seen, was not merely his
technique; it was his moral principle also. Gandhi did not
place much emphasis on the results of his actions, for his
commitment was to the eternal moral principles of truth and
nonviolence. Many a time, Gandhi acted at the risk of becoming
"unpopular," and in the face of seething opposition. "A
leader," he said, "is useless when he acts against the prompting
of his own conscience, surrounded as he must be by people
holding all kinds of views. He will drift like an anchorless
ship, if he has not the inner voice to hold him firm and guide
him."[16]

Leadership involves decision making, and Gandhi was sometimes accused of being an autocratic decision maker. Yet, if he
appeared to others as an autocrat, Gandhi thought of his actions as a defense of fundamental moral principle. When he
was unmoved by the arguments of his followers, it was trans-
parently clear that Gandhi sincerely believed his followers to
be mistaken. Nehru admits that this was often the case. "Bapu

(Gandhi) had a curious knack of doing the right thing at the psychological moment, and it might be that his action—impossible to justify as it was from my point of view—would lead to great results, not only in the narrow field it was confined, but in the wider aspects of our national struggle."[17] Gandhi knew the people of India and their aspirations far better than his followers did. Nehru again concedes: "Always we had the feeling that, while we might be more logical, Gandhi knew India far better than we did."[18]

What saved Gandhi's image as a democrat was the fact that he never approached people or problems in an impersonal, organizational manner. He was always on a person-to-person basis. No one went away from a conference with Gandhi with the impression that Gandhi had not given him sincere and respectful attention. When his followers gave obedience to distasteful direction, their obedience was combined with respect and trust. "What a magician, I thought," said Nehru, "was this little man sitting in Yeravada prison, and how well he knew how to pull strings that move people's hearts!"[19]

The remarkable thing about Gandhi's leadership is that he retained the trust and respect of so many followers over such a long period of time. There were many years of false starts, of compromises and stinging defeats. There were decades of uncertainty about the ultimate success of the cause. Of course, defections occurred. But there were always followers who credited Gandhi's rigidity in making unpopular decisions to his moral principles, whereas his compromises were interpreted as prudential judgments of circumstances.

Thus it was that Gandhi, whether rigid or flexible, never seemed to be "out of character." His unpredictable responses were not interpreted as irresponsibility, but as the paradoxical mystique of a great man. Gandhi was, as Nehru put it, "an extraordinary pardox. I suppose all outstanding men are to some extent."[20] E. Stanley Jones, in an eloquent passage, brings out this paradoxical nature of Gandhi:

> Gandhi seemed very simple, and yet he was very complex. He was a meeting place of East and West, and

yet represented the soul of the East; he was an urban
man who became the voice of the peasant masses; he
was passive and militant, and both at one and the same
time; he was the ascetic and the servant, aloof from and yet
with the multitudes, and with them as their servant;
he was the mystical and the practical come to embodiment,
the man of prayer and the man of the spinning wheel
and ten thousand other practical things connected with
economic redemption; he combined the Hindu and the
Christian in himself, a Hindu at the center of his allegiance
and yet deeply Christianized; he was the simple and
the shrewd, the candid and the courteous; he combined the
serious and the playful, a man who could shake empires
and could tickle a child beneath the chin and gain a
laugh and a friend; he had poise, but not the poise of retreat
and aloofness; he had power to change situations by a
deep identification; he was strangely self-assertive; and
last of all, and perhaps the most important of all, he was
a person who embodied a cause—the cause of India's
freedom.[21]

A study of Gandhi's leadership qualities cannot overlook
the fact that while he exerted enormous authority over his
people, he seldom held any formal position or political office.
Nor was he ever interested in offices. His rise to leadership
was not through office. He had a great influence over people
because they loved, respected and trusted him. They were de-
voted to him because he spent his life in their service. It is
with these considerations in mind that we should examine
Gandhi's more explicit views on the qualities of leadership.

A Theory of Leadership

Leadership, it is sometimes contended, is not a peculiar
trait possessed by individuals. It is a relationship, the relation
of an individual to a group. It is interesting to note that the
"trait-theory" of leadership, which has come under attack by
political scientists in recent years, was discarded by Gandhi.

"I have all along believed," he said, "that what is possible for one is possible for all, my experiments have not been conducted in the closet, but in the open."[22] Nevertheless, it should be pointed out, that Gandhi recognized the unique position he was occupying. Despite his many disavowels of the authority that the title *Mahatma* suggests, he did issue a call to civil disobedience; and, later, when he felt that there had been a "Himalayan miscalculation," he called off the campaign that he had started. These acts indicate awareness of the peculiar responsibilities of a leader.

Although Gandhi was himself a leader, he did not have much of a theory of leadership. Usually he equates the word *"Satyagrahi"* with that of a "leader." As we have seen, the meaning of the word *"Satyagrahi"* is a "seeker after truth." The obligation to seek truth is not regarded as something which is enjoined on some, and not on others. It is a categorical imperative for everybody. Gandhi, therefore, occasionally gives the impression that his army consists only of generals with no soldiers, and that everyone is his own commander.

Gandhi, as we have noted, was a *"practical* idealist." He realized quite early that in the *Satyagraha* campaigns there should be a leader-follower relationship, unless the entire group wanted to pursue truth independently. Where this was not possible, it was proper for an individual to follow a fellow-traveller. The following discussion throws light on the problem:

Q. Must not the person wanting to pursue truth be of high moral and intellectual equipment?
A. (Gandhi): No. It would be impossible to expect that from every one. If A has evolved a truth by his own efforts which B, C and others are to accept, I should not require them to have the equipment of A.
Q. Then it comes to this that a man comes to a decision and others of lower intellectual and moral equipment would have to blindly follow him.
A. Not blindly. All I wish to urge is that each individual,

unless he wants to carry on his pursuit of truth independently, needs to follow someone who has determined truth.[23]

The fact that an individual has reached some truth, therefore, entitles him to be a leader, and, at the same time, obliges the group to follow him. And it is in this context that we can understand Gandhi's statement that a leader should not be a follower of his followers, but should be one who should hold firm to his conscience.

The question now arises as to what happens when two independent *Satyagrahis* arrive at different conclusions. While Gandhi never doubted that honestly striving after truth always leads to the same conclusions by any number of individuals, being imperfect, we apprehend truth with some limitations. Therefore, when truth appears differently to two leaders, they should not break each other's heads, but try to "convert" each other to their respective points of view. Leaders, therefore, should commit themselves firmly to nonviolence, not only to settle their own problems but also to settle problems with their opponents.

Looking back at our discussion so far, we see that some qualifications for leadership which Gandhi prescribes have already made their appearance. A leader, no less than his followers, is on a pilgrimage to truth. He is a leader because he has made more strides than his followers and is in a position to guide them. The fact that a leader is ahead of his followers implies that he has to be brave and courageous, and should take more risks and make more sacrifices. "The history of the world is full of instances of men who rose to leadership by sheer force of self-confidence, bravery and tenacity."[24] The leader should be firmly committed to nonviolence, and where there is a difference between himself and his followers, fellow-pilgrims or opponents, he should not coerce, but "convert" them to his point of view. Implied in the leader's commitment to nonviolence is his willingness to suffer and sacrifice, harboring no anger and enmity towards anyone, not insulting or committing assault even on his bitter opponents, and so on. As part of the constructive work, the leader should disseminate information as faithfully as possible, and should serve the people to the best of his ability. A leader, in fact, is not the boss, but the servant of the people.

Modern political scientists may be dismayed at this mixture of the spiritual, the moral and the practical elements in Gandhi's meager theory of leadership. Gandhi viewed all of these elements as a whole. For Gandhi, the spiritual is truly practical; the truly political is the truly moral and religious. "My life is one indivisible," he said, "and all my activities run into one another, and they all have their rise in my insatiable love of mankind."[25]

Gandhi did not believe that leaders are *born* with these qualifications. Leaders are to be made, and hence the continuing need for "experiments." Gandhi himself was credited with the fact that he "made heroes out of clay," inspiring superior performances by unpromising individuals. Though, in a sense, every man has to make himself a leader, still some kind of guidance is necessary, and Gandhi worked out an elaborate training program for leaders and sub-leaders in his *Ashram* life.

Organizational Theory

The leader-group approach also implies an organization through which the leader and the group work. Gandhi himself utilized the Indian National Congress for his propaganda and parliamentary purposes. Gandhi always took an interest in organizational matters, and one of his last testaments worked out a suitable constructive organization to ameliorate the social, moral and economic conditions of the Indian villages. For this purpose he suggested the following constitution. He called the suggested organization "*Lok Seva Sangh.*" Here are some of the proposals in his draft:

> Every *panchayat* of five adult men or women being villagers or village-minded shall form a unit.

Two such contiguous *panchayats* shall form a working party under a leader elected from among themselves.

When there are one hundred such *panchayats* the fifty first grade leaders shall elect from among themselves a second grade leader and so on, the first grade leaders meanwhile working under the second grade leader. Parallel groups of two hundred *panchayats* shall continue to be formed till they cover the whole of India, each succeeding group of *panchayats* electing a second grade leader after the manner of the first. All second grade leaders shall serve for the whole of India and severally for their respective areas. The second grade leaders may elect, whenever they deem necessary, from among themselves a chief who will during pleasure, regulate and command all the groups.[26]

This passage gives the impression that Gandhi was interested in a hierarchical structure of leadership from the local to the national level. We have already pointed out that he was not unaware of the unique position he was holding in national affairs. He also expected Jawaharlal Nehru to be his successor. "I have said for many years and I say now that not Rajaji but Jawaharlal will be my successor. He says that he does not understand my language, and that he speaks a language foreign to me. This may or may not be true. But language is no bar to a union of hearts. And I know this, when I am gone he will speak my language."[27]

It should, nevertheless, be pointed out that Gandhi's main concern was not with the making of national leaders, but with the training of local leaders. This is in consonance with his conception of India as a cluster of decentralized village units. Most of our problems, Gandhi seems to think, are local in character rather than national or international. Local leaders are important because they know the people better and can tackle their problems more effectively. If there is a constructive program, for example, it is the local people who are the beneficiaries; and, if there is a case of oppression, it is again the local people who are the victims. In terms of effectiveness, therefore, nothing succeeds like a movement led by local leaders. It is in this context that Gandhi advises the Jews that they should resort to *Satyagraha* against the Nazi regime with their own resources and not be dependent on outside help. Though Gandhi had a concept of what he called "sympathy *satyagraha*," he was generally not in favor of a band of roaming *Satyagrahis* to set right the injustices of the entire world. This is so because an oppressor can be "converted" and "weaned away" from evil only by the victim and not by an outside agency. Through external pressure, he may stop his oppressive acts, but he will not realize their essentially evil nature.

The Question of Effectiveness

The conventional test by which leaders are identified is implicit in the question: "Are they effective in influencing others?" For Gandhi this is an irrelevant question, since it presupposes that a leader has to achieve certain stated goals by any means. This is not the assumption with which he was working. It is not so much the actual attainment of ends that is important; *how* we achieve them is important. "They say 'means are after all means.' I would say 'means are after all everything.' As the means, so the end. There is no wall of separation between means and end. Indeed the Creator has given us control (and that too very limited) over means, none over the end. Realization of the goal is in exact proportion to that of the means. This is a proposition that admits of no exception."[28]

Even though Gandhi did not want to be judged in this manner, there is no denying the fact that he was successful, especially in bringing about a social awakening and in the social reconstruction work he had undertaken. Before Gandhi entered the Indian scene, efforts at gaining Indian independence were confined either to a few intellectuals who were agitating in a constitutional way for the rights of their countrymen, or to some revolutionaries who were planning an armed overthrow. Gandhi changed the entire nature of the struggle, from that of a constitutional debate to a people's direct action, and from a violent to a nonviolent movement. It was no mean achievement to make some four hundred million people conscious of themselves as a nation and involve them in a nonviolent struggle. As Nehru says:

> Gandhiji's stress was never on the intellectual approach to a problem but on character and piety. He did succeed amazingly in giving backbone and character to the Indian people.
> It was this extraordinary stiffening up of the masses that filled us with confidence. A demoralized, backward, and broken-up people suddenly straightened their backs and lifted their heads and took part in disciplined, joint action on a country-wide scale. This action itself, we felt, would give irresistible power to the masses.[29]

In the field of social justice, likewise, one discerns the profound impact of Gandhian thought. Not only did social attitudes change on such problems as untouchability and the emancipation of women, these principles were also incorporated in the new Indian Constitution. So far there is general agreement.

What is disputed, however, is whether Indian independence was due to the nonviolent struggle that Gandhi undertook. Was Gandhi able to make his followers accept nonviolence as a creed? The answer to this seems to be a hesitant "no." Gandhi's immediate follower, Nehru, accepted nonviolence as a technique, and so did the Congress organization. "What I admired," said Nehru, "was the moral and ethical side of our movement and of *Satyagraha*. I did not give an absolute allegiance to the doctrine of nonviolence or accept it forever, but it attracted me more and more, and the belief grew upon me that, situated as we were in India and with our background and traditions, it was the right policy for us. . . . A worthy end should have worthy means leading up to it. That seemed not only a good ethical doctrine but sound, practical politics, for the means that are not good often defeat the end in view and raise new problems and difficulties."[30]

When India was partitioned and there were communal disturbances on a vast scale, Gandhi said: "It is true that the nonviolence that we practised was the nonviolence of the weak, i.e., no non-violence at all. But I maintain that this was not what I presented to my countrymen. Nor did I present to them the weapon of non-violence because they were weak or disarmed or without military training."[31] But even if he is viewed as developing a technique or a weapon, Gandhi should still be credited with the fact that he kept the struggle going for a long time in a nonviolent way.

The end of this struggle having been Indian independence, the question arises whether independence came as the result of Gandhi's efforts. The British Historian, Arnold Toynbee, attributes the achievement not only to the efforts of Gandhi but also to the Indian people's nonviolent spirit. These two spirits were combined in a novel expression of the ancient Indian heritage.[32] On the other hand, an eminent Indian historian, R. C. Majumdar, doubts this. According to him, "that Gandhi played a very great role in rousing the political consciousness of the masses nobody can possibly deny. But it would be a travesty of truth to give him the sole credit for the freedom of India, and sheer nonsense to look upon *Satyagraha* (or *charkha*, according to some) as the unique weapon by which it was achieved."[33] In the ultimate analysis, many factors contributed to the British withdrawal.

Also relevant to the question of Gandhi's effectiveness was his impact upon the issue of Hindu-Moslem unity. His handling of the problem, it is often pointed out, was sentimental rather than realistic. His magic wand did not cast a spell on the Muslim League, and Gandhi could not "convert" Jinnah from demanding the partition of India on communal and religious grounds. According to Professor Majumdar, again, Gandhi "accepted, as fact, a purely imaginary fraternity, and completely ignored the fundamental differences between the

Hindus and Muslims based on history, culture and tradition."[34] Majumdar, no doubt, credits Gandhi with the fact that "though he failed, his earnest and life-long devotion . . . evokes our highest admiration, and his precept and example will always be stored as priceless treasures in India."[35]

Thus while doubts have been expressed on the wisdom of Gandhi's "spiritualized politics," the course of events during the phase of Gandhi's life and after his death makes one dubious concerning the extent of his influence. Contemporary India, it is said, is not the India that Gandhi envisioned. His dream was to make the country decentralized and village-oriented, whereas present-day India is tending more and more towards centralization and urbanization. Big machinery scared him, but the slogan nowadays is "Industrialize or perish." Gandhi supported the trusteeship idea of capitalism, but the creed of modern India is socialism and state-ownership. Spiritualized politics" was the keynote of Gandhian thought, whereas some form of power politics is accepted as a fact of life by the present Indian government.

These last comments, naturally, do not tell us what Gandhi would have done in 1950 or in 1969, if he had not been struck down and if he could have retained full vigor until his centenary. They tell us that Gandhi, while he was alive and active, did not surround himself with yes-men, nor did he solve all problems.

Gandhi's leadership qualities, while he was alive, were attested by the transformation of servile, down-at-the-heels masses into a confident and disciplined movement. If he did not win India's independence as quickly as Washington won ours, it must be said that no shots were fired on his orders. If he did not destroy the caste system as quickly as Lincoln destroyed slavery, it must be said that the untouchables won legal rights without a civil war. Gandhi's influence in his own time was evident in the success of a difficult undertaking, requiring devotion and self-restraint on the part of literally millions of human beings.

The record of that leadership is inspiring to all who hope

for the nonviolent resolution of future conflicts. At the same time, it is a record that is disturbing to educators and to others who put their trust in education; for, although Gandhi's role was often that of a teacher, there are few suggestions in the story of his own development for school men who would like to turn out future Gandhis.

4

Gandhi on Education

IF GANDHI does not tell educators how to produce future Gandhis, he does, nevertheless, have a great deal to say about education. Few people outside India are familiar with his efforts in the educational field. Those efforts were considerable and they were made, almost continuously, for something like forty years. They were undertaken on the theory that no social reform is possible without reformation of individual persons. Although he regarded personal reformation as always, in some sense, a personal achievement, he thought that proper teaching would be helpful.

Being an activist, Gandhi did not write about education with the neatness that is attained by scholars who have time to polish carefully worded manuscripts. His thoughts on the subject were dashed off between engagements, some of the engagements not being invitational affairs. Many of his most interesting comments were incidental to his "experiments" in the establishment of informal schools. As early as 1904 he was conducting educational experiments; first in the Phoenix Settlement near Durban, and in the Tolstoy Farm in Transvaal, South Africa. They were repeated in the *Sabarmati Ashram* and the *Satyagraha Ashram* in India.

Gandhi's thinking on education had its roots in his revolt against the classical tradition in Indian education which, along with all the good things it had to offer, confined itself to teaching the fortunate few. Gandhi also objected to formal English education which, in his opinion, had a purely utilitarian objective. English education was introduced in India in 1835 through the efforts of Lord Macaulay with the aim of overcoming the language barrier between the British rulers and Indian subjects. It was intended that a small subordinate staff should thus be trained for administration. Although the study of the English language by itself was not regarded by Gandhi as wholly an evil, the system of English education was alien to Indian society and disruptive in its effects. It created new class distinctions between the "English-knowing" and "non-English-knowing" population, and in actual practice did not touch Indian society except for a microscopic minority. "It was conceived and born in error, for the English rulers honestly believed the indigenous system to be worse than useless. It has been nurtured in sin, for the tendency has been to dwarf the Indian body, mind and soul."[1]

Gandhi had a firm faith in the democratic equality of all men, and the system of education he conceived was not to be the monopoly of an elite; it was to be the right of all. Such a democratization of education posed a great challenge, especially for one who was working in the context of Indian society where the majority of people were poor and illiterate. Literacy, Gandhi thought, could not be the primary goal of the kind of education that the people needed most, though it would be helpful. Emphasis on literacy and book-learning made the child a passive spectator instead of an active participant. "We have up to now concentrated on stuffing children's minds with all kinds of information, without ever thinking of stimulating or developing them. Let us now cry a halt and concentrate on educating the child properly through manual work, not as a side activity, but as the prime means of intellectual training."[2] Any education, he emphasized, should be such that it is child-oriented rather than subject-oriented, and it should be an integral part of life, and not something divorced from life.

Craft-Oriented Education

Gandhi hit upon the idea of a "craft-oriented" education. He says:

> I would therefore, begin the child's education by
> teaching it a useful handicraft and enabling it to produce
> from the moment it begins its training. I hold that
> the highest development of the mind and the soul is
> possible under such a system of education. Only every
> handicraft has to be taught not merely mechanically as is
> done today but scientifically, i.e., the child should know
> the why and the wherefore of every process.[3]

The crafts that Gandhi recommended for the purpose are rural handicrafts like spinning and weaving, carpentry, pounding paddy, oil-pressing, tanning, match-making, *Khadi* (handspun cloth), etc. The teaching of handicraft to the child should not be construed merely as a part of the educational practice, but it should be the pivot.

The advantages of adopting this method are twofold. First, it breaks down the dualism between brain and brawn, between intellectual work and manual labor, in that the development of intellect will itself be dependent upon the learning of a handicraft. Gandhi points out:

> The utterly false idea that intelligence can be developed
> only through book-reading should give place to the
> truth that the quickest development of the mind can
> be achieved by the artisan's work being learnt in a scientific
> manner. True development of the mind commences
> immediately the apprentice is taught at every step why
> a particular manipulation of the hand or a tool is required.[4]

Secondly, the child will be an active participant in the whole learning process, and takes great pride in what he is doing.

It might appear to a casual reader that Gandhi's views on education are purely vocation-oriented. Far from it. Education as a means to find a vocation in later life is only part of his social reconstruction program. In fact, Gandhi defines education as "an all-round drawing out of the best in child and man—body, mind and spirit,"[5] and this, he hopes to achieve by making craft central to his system. The craft is only the medium through which the whole education of the body, the mind, and the soul develops.

What is commonly known in America as "progressive education" is akin to this approach, and it is interesting to note that Gandhi, who was not well-read in "theories" of education, was in some agreement with these educationists. The differences between the progressive education movement and the Gandhian movement are in the purposes the two movements aim to achieve. For the progressive educationists, a child-centered education which takes into account the needs and interests of the child is in tune with the democratic spirit, in that the child is treated as an end in himself; and, such education itself leads to the strengthening of democracy. The Gandhian conception, while not denying this objective, had somewhat different objectives as we shall now see.

Gandhi was alarmed and distressed by the way in which the autonomous village economy was disappearing in the wake of industrialization. The industrialization of England and large-scale dumping of cheap goods on India resulted in a growing unemployment among villagers who were on the verge of starvation.

Before the British advent, India spun and wove, in her millions of cottages, just the supplement she needed for adding to her meagre agricultural resources. This cottage industry, so vital for India's existence, has been ruined by incredibly heartless and inhuman processes, as described by English witnesses. Little do town dwellers know how the semi-starved masses of India are slowly sinking to lifelessness. Little do they know that their miserable comfort represents the brokerage they get for the work they do for the foreign exploiter, that the profits and the brokerage are sucked from the masses. Little do they realize that the Government established by law in British India is carried on for this exploitation of the masses. No sophistry, no jugglery in figures, can explain away the evidence that the skeletons in many villages present to the naked eye. I have no doubt whatsoever that both England and the town dwellers of India will have to answer, if there is a God above, for this crime against humanity, which is perhaps unequalled in history.[6]

What, then, was to be done? The solution, he thought, did not lie in more industrialization where there might be plenty for all and where people need not toil. The problem essentially was one of restoring the self-sufficiency of the village economy. His message, therefore, was "the gospel of rural-mindedness." "I want to resuscitate the village of India. Today our villages have become a mere appendage to the cities. They exist, as it were, to be exploited by the latter and depend on the latter's sufferance. This is unnatural. It is only when the cities realize the duty of making an adequate return to the villages for the strength and sustenance which they derive from them, instead of selfishly exploiting them, that a healthy and moral relationship between the two will spring up."[7]

The problems of industrialization and large-scale unemployment were not just economic problems for Gandhi. They were moral problems as well. "I must confess," he said elsewhere, "that I do not draw a sharp or any distinction between economics and ethics. Economics that hurts the moral well-being of an individual or a nation is immoral and therefore, sinful. Thus, the economics that permits one country to prey upon another [is] immoral."[8] Gandhi was objecting to an industrialization based on exploitation, the exploitation of one individual by another, the exploitation of the villages by the cities, and the exploitation of one nation by another.

Now, if we view Gandhi's emphasis on a craft-centered education against the background of this moral economy, its implication for his social philosophy become clear. First of all, such an education will be self-supporting in nature; "in fact, self-support is the acid test of its reality."[9] Why does Gandhi insist that education be self-supporting, and what does he mean by it? Gandhi means by "self-support" 1) that the craft a child learns in the school enables him to support himself in later life. It is socially "useful" in the sense that it acts as a kind of insurance for the child when he grows up. 2) Secondly, the school itself would be self-supporting, in that the salaries of the teachers at least could be paid out of the sale of the articles that the children manufacture. "The introduction of manual training will serve a double purpose in a poor country like ours. It will pay for the education of our children and teach them an occupation on which they can fall back in afterlife, if they choose for earning a living."[10]

Since most of the activities in the school, in which the child is a partner, are performed in groups, the training fosters in him a cooperative spirit and social responsibility. He will become aware of his duties as a member of the society. From the performance of duties there will arise the individual's rights.

Craft-oriented education, furthermore, teaches the child the dignity of labor and eliminates the age-old prejudice against manual work. In the context of Indian society, this would break down the traditional division of society into different castes.

Finally, and this is the most important aspect of Gandhian educational thought, exploitation and the extinction of the village handicrafts by industrialization will come to a halt. The child who develops a liking for the rural handicrafts and the rural-mindedness refuses to be exploited, and exploitation, to Gandhi, is the essence of violence. Moreover:

> if the city children are to play their part in this great and noble work of social reconstruction, the vocations through which they are to achieve their education ought to be directly related to the requirements of the villages. So far as I can see, the various processes of cotton manufacture from the ginning and cleaning of cotton to the spinning of yarn answer this test as nothing else does. . . .
> My plan to impart Primary Education through the medium of village handicrafts like spinning and carding, etc. is thus conceived as the spear-head of a silent social revolution fraught with the most far-reaching consequences.

It will provide a healthy and moral basis of relationship
between the city and the village and will thus go a
long way towards eradicating some of the worst evils of
the present social insecurity and poisoned relationship
between the classes. It will check the progressive decay
of our villages and lay the foundation of a juster social
order in which there is no unnatural division between the
"haves" and the "have-nots" and everybody is assured
of a living wage and the right to freedom. And all this
would be accomplished without the horror of a bloody class
war or a colossal capital expenditure such as would be
involved in the mechanization of a vast continent like
India. Nor would it entail a helpless dependence on
foreign imported machinery or technical skill. Lastly, by
obviating the necessity of highly specialized talent, it
would place the destiny of the masses, as it were, in
their own hands. But who will bell the cat? Will the cityfolk
listen to me at all? Or, will mine remain a mere cry in
the wilderness?[11]

Nehru's Education for Industrialization

In India during Gandhi's own life time his call did remain
a cry in the wilderness. Jawaharlal Nehru, who was next only
to Gandhi in his influence, did not accept the "gospel of rural-
mindedness" or the slogan "back to the rural economy." "That
remedy," Nehru said, "might well be worse than the disease."[12]
Instead he proposed that the cities and the villages should be
more closely linked than hitherto, and that the economic and
cultural level of the villages should be raised to that of the
cities. Nehru pointed out that "it should be possible to organize
modern industry in such a way as to keep men and women, as
far as possible, in touch with the land, and to raise the cultural level of the rural areas. The village and the city should
approach each other in regard to life's amenities, so that in both
there should be full opportunities for bodily and mental development and a full all-rounded life."[13]

In Nehru's opinion the bringing together of the towns and villages by close links, and the improvement of the lot of villages, involves the introduction of cottage and small scale industries in the rural areas, and, to some extent, heavy industry as well.

Thus even the enthusiastic advocates for cottage and small-scale industries recognize that big-scale industry is, to a certain extent, necessary and inevitable; only they would like to limit it as far as possible. Superficially then the question becomes one of emphasis and adjustment of the two forms of production and economy. It can hardly be challenged that, in the context of the modern world, no country can be politically and economically independent, even within the framework of international inter-dependence, unless it is highly industrialized and has developed its power resources to the utmost. Nor can it achieve or maintain high standards of living and liquidate poverty without the aid of modern technology in almost every sphere of life. An industrially backward country will continually upset the world equilibrium and encourage the aggressive tendencies of more developed countries.[14]

A little farther on, Nehru says that "if technology demands the big machine, as it does today in a large measure, then the big machine with all its implications and consequences must be accepted. Where it is possible, in terms of technology, to decentralize production, this would be desirable."[15]

Gandhi, nevertheless, insisted that a nonviolent social structure can only be established by decentralizing the economy and recognizing the autonomy of the village units. Simple village homes need no protection and policing, for there is nothing to take away from them. Centralization and industrialization, on the contrary, require a big police force. A huge factory, for example, must have adequate security arrangements because of a perennial danger of being robbed. In spite of innumerable foreign invasions, India and its culture had survived because of its rural decentralization. Gandhi also was convinced that rurally organized India would be in a better position to defend itself against future attacks than would an urbanized India, whatever the size of its armed forces.

In the decentralized village unit, Gandhi sees the human community at its best. It will be the perfect community which is guided by mutual trust and confidence, where every member will earn his living by his own honest toil without coercion and exploitation. Gandhi's economic constitution is such

> that no one under it should suffer from want of food and clothing. In other words everybody should be able to get sufficient work to enable him to make the two ends meet. And this ideal can be universally realized only if the means of production of the elementary necessaries of life remain in the control of the masses. These should be freely available to all as God's air and water are or ought to be; they should not be made a vehicle of traffic for the exploitation of others.[16]

In this decentralized village unit, each member of the community is an autonomous moral agent, firmly committed to nonviolence; and each respects the other members as ends in themselves.

Decentralization is not confined to the economic sphere alone, but also affects the political sphere as well.

> Political power means capacity to regulate national life through national representatives. If the national life becomes so perfect as to become self-regulated, no representation becomes necessary. There is then a state of enlightened anarchy. In such a state every one is his own ruler. He rules himself in such a manner that he is never a hindrance to his neighbour. In the ideal State, therefore, there is no political power because there is no State.[17]

We have so far dwelt on the social aspect of education and its objectives. The "whole education" of the child is, however, not exhausted in the duties that he renders society. Gandhi recognizes the uniqueness and individuality of each child. Professor Axtelle put the idea very well in another connection: "Individualization is itself a function of socialization; it is defining for one's self, one's unique and peculiar role in varied social relations."[18]

Does the teaching of the craft by itself lead to the ideal society that Gandhi conceived, or is something more required? Gandhi never claimed that the teaching of the craft, even in the most scientific manner, is the whole education of the child. Some other elements are also essential.

Moral Education

Regarding the cultural aspect of education, Gandhi says: "I attach for more importance to the cultural aspect of education than to the literary. Culture is the foundation, the primary thing."[19] Gandhi distinguishes between the "culture of the mind" and the "culture of the heart" and says that the former must be subservient to the latter. Now the "culture of the heart" is, for Gandhi, nothing other than morality or character building. He says further: "I had always given the first place to the culture of the heart or the building of character, and, as I felt confident that moral training could be given to all alike, no matter how different their ages and their upbringing, I decided to live amongst them."[20] More than on anything else, Gandhi places great emphasis on the moral aspect of education. "All our learning or recitation of the *Vedas*, correct knowledge of Sanskrit, Latin, Greek and what not will avail us nothing if they do not enable us to cultivate absolute purity of heart. The end of all knowledge must be building up of character."[21] Elsewhere, addressing a student gathering he said: "Your education is absolutely worthless, if it is not built on a solid foundation of truth and purity. If you, boys, are not careful about the personal purity of your lives and if you are not careful about being pure in thought, speech, and deed, then I tell you that you are lost, although you may become perfect finished scholars."[22] The moral life and the development of good character are possible only in a disciplined life, and Gandhi insists therefore on the restraint of our desires, passions, etc. It is at this point that Gandhi's view of the moral life merges with that of the religious life.

For Gandhi, morality and religion are convertible terms. A moral life divorced from religious truth is like a house built upon sand. Moreover, "as soon as we lose the moral basis, we cease to be religious. There is no such thing as religion overriding morality. Man for instance cannot be untruthful, cruel and incontinent and claim to have God on his side."[23] He vigorously argues for the introduction of religious instruction in schools, therefore. "Religion" however does not mean an organized religion for Gandhi but a firm commitment to Truth. "Let me explain what I mean by religion. It is not the Hindu religion, which I certainly prize above all other religions, but the religion which transcends Hinduism, which changes one's very nature, which binds one indissolubly to the Truth within and which ever purifies."[24] Truth for Gandhi *is* God, and nonviolence is the means to attain Truth. And one who has realized Truth has also realized his Self.

The Universities

Unlike educators who think that the role of primary and secondary education is different from that of college and university education, Gandhi sees a continuity in all phases of education. University education, he says, must be "an extension and continuation of the basic education course,"[25] and should be directed towards the welfare of the community. "Today," he complained," the youth educated in our universities either ran after government jobs or fell into devious ways and sought outlet for their frustration by fomenting unrest. . . . The aim of university education should be to turn out true servants of the people."[26]

Gandhi was against the establishment of universities financed out of State revenues, unless they were based on "realities." "To be based on realities is to be based on national, *i.e.*, State, requirements. And the State will pay for it."[27] Otherwise, "it is criminal to pay for a training which benefits neither the nation nor the individual. In my opinion there is no such thing as individual benefit which cannot be proved to be also national benefit."[28]

In general, however, Gandhi says that all higher education should be financed solely out of private endowments. Higher technical and professional education should not be the concern of universities, but should be undertaken by the industries themselves under the supervision of universities. Universities should not act as a clearance house for industry.

There remains, therefore, nontechnical higher education, about which Gandhi is emphatic that it should be financed by the public. "In my opinion," he says, "it is not for a democratic State to find money for founding universities. If the people want them, they will supply the funds. Universities so founded will adorn the country which they represent."[29] He adds further: "A university never needs a pile of majestic buildings and treasures of gold and silver. What it does need most of all is the intelligent backing of public opinion."[30] Now the university can expect public backing when it works not in isolation and in ivory towers, but when it shows a certain concern and responsibility for the community and its problems. "It is my settled conviction," Gandhi said, "that no deserving institution ever dies for want of support. Institutions that have died have done so either because there was nothing in them to commend them to the public or because those in control lost faith, or which is perhaps the same thing, lost stamina."[31]

A number of Gandhi's statements may remind Americans of the New England Transcendentalists and their conception of a good education. Like Emerson, for example, Gandhi objected to a schooling that left the graduates servile, unimaginative, and obsessed by immediate desires and aversions. He wanted to help children develop self-reliance, a self-reliance in seeking something larger than themselves. And, also like Emerson, Gandhi expected this self-reliant idealism to diminish the need for the coercive powers of the State.

The specific educational practices recommended by Gandhi should not, of course, be regarded as models for all time to come, nor should the practices that he denounced be taken as description of what is going on everywhere. What he recommended were "experiments" that were possible under the conditions of his day. He denounced certain practices that existed in the context of colonialism. If there are, in Gandhi's educational views, any principles that are deserving of general application, they must be stated in such a way as to permit teachers and pupils who face different conditions to work out their own "experiments." Perhaps, the only general principles of education are Gandhi's oft-repeated assertions about ends and means. The pursuit of human ends involves a person in social conflicts. In these conflicts everyone can be helped to learn that he has a choice of means. The nonviolent means are not only instrumental in avoiding war; they are also the way to self-improvement.

TWO

American Responses

5

What Can a Dead Gandhi Do for Live Americans?

It is one thing to honor the memory of Gandhi by recalling the record of his career. It is quite another thing to honor his memory by emulating his example as we try to work out our own careers. There is a peculiar difficulty in seeking guidance from the history of a leader such as Gandhi. The difficulty was stated by Dr. Brock Chisholm, when he was consulted about the future of Hull House, the settlement house that Jane Addams had founded eighty years earlier:

> We have an unfortunate tendency to freeze our great prophets at the moment of their death. This, I think, is a very unfortunate human tendency. All our great prophets were rebels in their time and rebelled against the orthodoxies in which they were born. They all advocated changing established behavior patterns to fit the new circumstances that had arisen. They were all prophets of change. If they were alive now, I am sure that they would still be rebels against the orthodoxies that surrounded them—that they would still be insisting on change—that they would not be the same persons they were when they died. . . . To go back to our prophets for guidance is, I believe, not to do honor to our prophets, except to the degree of recognizing that they were people who demanded change.[1]

Some such warning is needed to keep pious admirers from making the occasional expedients of great leaders into general rules to be followed slavishly in all times and places. Gandhi, for example, had a good reason for not riding in first class railroad carriages. But that does not make the refusal to ride first class virtuous for all time to come.

Dr. Chisholm overstated his case, however, when he objected to any specific guidance by our prophets. Gandhi's relating of personal purity and integrity to public affairs, to mention only one of his insights, was something that few human beings have achieved. Granting that we are not today in Gandhi's sandals, we may still hope for some guidance through a retracing of the steps that he took in his "experiments."

Furthermore, we find in the record of Gandhi's life a persistent effort to remind people of standards which they tend to forget in the heat of battle or in the depths of despair. The reminders are often resented. As one of our American lawyers has observed:

> No rage is equal to the rage of a contented right-thinking
> man when he is confronted in the market place by an
> idea which belongs in the pulpit.[2]

But Gandhi's ability to recall forgotten pledges and goals was eventually appreciated by his associates and even by some of his adversaries. He had the ability to "think otherwise." The rhetoric that he used in overcoming obsessions and hysteria is, therefore, a permanent addition to the world's "wisdom" literature.

A Gandhian "System?"

It is a temptation for philosophers and theologians to formulate the "essence" of Gandhi's teachings. Rising above the particular remedies that Gandhi recommended for particular circumstances, they seek, in the statement of some very general and abstract criterion, *the* principle that was always being applied. No doubt, such studies are sometimes enlightening, as they are in the work of Arne Naess, who found in Gandhi's comments a consistent devotion to "self-realization."[3] But such epitomizations, like Gandhi's own efforts to summarize his philosophy, take the edge off many incisive declarations. And, when generalizations are offered as substitutes for a reading of Gandhi's biography, they are expected to do too much. Although some moral and religious ideas are hard to grasp, the peculiar power of most of such ideas comes from their being injected into a situation where attention is riveted on something else. The detailed story of Gandhi's life is full of sudden and unexpected juxtapositions of matters that at first seem to be irrelevant, yet on second thought are vitally related. Gandhi's daring sensitivity is not fully preserved in abstract formulas. Thus it is, that men of a later time, confronted by novel conditions, may have more chances of emulating his example in their own lives, if they can recall the examples.

American Difficulties

For Americans, of course, it is not merely the passage of time that makes it difficult to "follow Gandhi." Some Americans have never experienced the greatest evils to which Gandhi was exposed. Very few have even a bare acquaintance with India's traditions. The moral and religious heritage, which Gandhi both preserved and modified, is for them an alien ideology. In some respects, it is repugnant to people of European and African background. Before attempting a Gandhian critique of any American practices, it is fitting, therefore, that the differences between American and Indian life should be emphasized. With all due respect for the memory of the Reverend Martin Luther King, it is quite possible that he and his followers did too much imitating of what Gandhi had done and not enough Gandhian searching of the souls of Americans.

To single out one striking difference between Indian and western traditions, there is nothing in the West that is comparable to the sacredness of subhuman life. The Society for the

Prevention of Cruelty to Animals, a nineteenth century American creation, might be taken as an expression of the non-violence principle, but that was not the case. The SPCA was primarily opposed to needless suffering and, to that end, has participated in the mercy killing of unwanted animals. Someone who is skilled in the making of scholastic distinctions could dismiss this difference as trivial. ("After all, Gandhi's great work was in dealing with the unjust treatment of *human* beings.") Yet, this difference is a symptom of a profound contrast in the orientation of Western and Indian feelings.

The most obvious reason for not expecting an American Gandhi to be an exact replica of the Indian Gandhi is the unlikeness of the dominant social and political systems. The contrast between Gandhi's environment in 1919 and Martin Luther King's context in the 1960's may seem to be unimportant. Were not the rapid social changes in both cases part of the industrialization of the world? Was not the cry of "Injustice!" raised in each instance on behalf of people who were being victimized rather than benefited by the development of large-scale industry? Did not King speak out for the agricultural laborers who had been displaced by mechanization and who were not being employed in factories and offices? Was his protest not comparable to Gandhi's plea for handicraftsmen bereft of the old subsistence economy without a share in the profits of British-based factories? Were not both of them saying that the machine should be the servant of man instead of man's being the slave of a machine?

Yes, but the evils that the Indian Gandhi was made aware of were the evils of a colonial empire that exploited India as a source of cheap raw materials and as a market. India was a country of villages that was being brought into an international economy on very unfavorable terms. Present-day America, by contrast, is more highly industrialized than the Britain that Gandhi criticized. The great majority of Americans live in cities or suburbs, and their breadwinners receive a portion of the largest Gross National Product of all time. It is true that the United States harbors a minority that is as depressed and oppressed as Gandhi's Indians, but an American Gandhi finds himself championing the cause, not of a majority, but of a minority. His principal opposition comes, not from foreigners overseas, but from "the people."

It is with such an awareness of the novelty of today's problems that admirers of Gandhi should think about attacking America's evils. There is nothing inherently and intrinsically right in a boycott. There is no assurance that a hunger strike or an unauthorized march will be everywhere and under all conditions a tactic worthy of a Gandhi. Those who wish to follow a master by exactly imitating what he did should choose a master who was less intelligent, less unpredictable than Gandhiji.

With these qualifications, it may be contended that a dead Gandhi can do something for live Americans.

6

What Can be Done For and With Non-Industrial Man?

HERE ARE some 1969 Americans who are trying to see their duty with Gandhian eyes. They see human beings who have been left out of a rich, productive, industrial economy. They see human beings who are being pushed around, unable apparently to make use of the protections and remedies of a "civil rights democracy."

How do these would-be Gandhians define their problem? How do they translate an uneasy conscience into a program of action? Will they not focus their attention upon the industrialization of our society? Will they not ask what they can do about people who have been left out in the transition to specialized, mechanized, automated production?

Recalling that Gandhi always kept in mind who he was and how his own activities were related to public evils, we should also identify our own status and (hopefully) the point of departure for anything that needs to be done. We, who write and (probably) most of you who read these pages are teachers and students. We are connected with educational institutions, and the first step in clarifying our problem would seem to be the identification of the schools' relation to the process of industrialization.

Although our schools originated in a preindustrial, agrarian age, they have—with much pulling and hauling—adjusted to the rapidly changing requirements of industry. The entire educational system can be viewed as the personnel department of the American economy. From bottom to top, there is a recruiting or selecting process, culminating in a decision either to recommend or not to recommend the student for specialized work. In the universities more and more of the instructors teach and do research in subjects that enable them to move from the university to industry or government and back again. As Professor Galbraith observes, "the new industrial state" has a corporate "technostructure," an "organized intelligence," in which only those who are capable of acquiring sophisticated technical skills can participate.[1]

Not very many of us are the avowed agents of industrial production, typified by engineering professors who attract corporations to industrial parks adjacent to the university campus. Nor do many of us "spin off' consulting companies that can enter into multimillion dollar contracts.[2] Nevertheless, as Professor George Counts said some years ago:

> Technology impresses its special character on a culture
> and on the bodies, minds, and hearts of those who use it.
> To think of technology solely in terms of its material
> products, of its discoveries and inventions, would be a
> grave mistake. In essence, it is a process, a way of working,
> a method of attacking problems, a mode of viewing the
> world.[3]

One evidence of the impact of specialized industry on education is the specialization of studies at the higher levels of schooling. Conway Zirkle once suggested that the Ph.D. degree diploma should read: "The Blank University certifies that ———knows nothing except Biochemistry." Specialization occurs, not merely in the sciences, but throughout the university, even in the "humanities." If a professor identifies himself as a teacher of literature or history, it is not impertinent to ask, "On what period do you specialize?" And, if a graduate student says that he is in Philosophy, he can expect to be asked, "What field of philosophy?"

The Drop-Outs

In this educational world, with its fine division of labor, it is easy to forget the children who drop out. The grades, certificates and letters of recommendation are all for the benefit of those who have the aptitudes, the health and the emotional make-up needed by employees and managers in a functional organization. In admitting the existence of this selectivity, we do not imply that the high-skill products of our schools should be levelled down. The graduates who win Nobel Prizes make contributions to the welfare of mankind. But, we have to admit, the schools seem to be singularly useless to those who are not candidates for the occupations in which Nobel Prizes are awarded. The prospect of a population divided into high-skill and no-skill castes has an unpleasant similarity to the Anglo-Indian system that Gandhi abhorred.

For us, then, the question is, "What are we going to do about the children who fail, who drop out, or who never get started in our employee-producing schools?" At this moment we are asking ourselves particularly what we are going to do about the children who are descendents of Africans who were brought to America as slaves. They, like many Indian and Spanish-American children, seldom enjoy either the preschool experience or the out-of-school environment which a technology-dominated education presupposes. But there are other children who also do not fit into the picture. There are the physically handicapped and those whose emotional maturation does not occur within the normal years of schooling.[4] There are also, at the college level, foreign students from underdeveloped countries, especially the countries that are not developing and won't be able to make good use of specialists in any case.* Another grouping of disadvantaged children (including many of those

---

* Female students are sometimes included in this list of children for whom the educational cupboard is bare; but special pleading may be suspected when that indictment is made. Quite apart from the increasing employment of women, the fact is that wives have important functions in an industrialized society and probably make as much use of an education as do their husbands.

just mentioned) consists of the residents of economically depressed areas, some of them remaining in rural areas where agricultural laborers and miners displaced by mechanization have not found satisfactory employment; others, migrating to urban ghettos.

The Choice of Targets

If we seriously intend a Gandhian attack upon the inequality of educational opportunities, we are looking for programs of organized, collective action. Obviously, any educator can find little tasks by which he, as an individual, can make a contribution. The puzzler is to locate some crucial large scale steps that can be helped along by a movement, and, if necessary, by *Satyagraha*. When, during and after the Second World War, the first serious attention was given to the problems, there were some relatively easy targets, viz., state laws and the policies of school boards that discriminated against certain children on account of their race. The repeal of these discriminatory admission policies was not easy; in some regions this struggle drags on; but it was easy to see that they were a proper target.

When, however, race was no longer a legal bar to admission into school, few children from the disadvantaged areas were finishing secondary schools, fewer still were getting university degrees; and the unequal participation in American industry was clearly being perpetuated by something other than discriminatory statutes and policies. For the vast majority of black students, as for the poor white students of "Appalachia," part of the trouble was the poverty and often the illiteracy of their parents. These children suffered from inadequate preschool training, from inadequate motivations, and from attendance in the poor schools of the urban and rural slums. But what should be the target of Gandhian agitation?

Dr. King selected residential segregation as one of his targets. After some legal obstacles to open housing had been overcome, demonstrations were organized for the purpose of

71

opening to Negroes certain all-white suburbs. Cicero, a suburb of Chicago, was selected as the target. With police protection the marchers braved the taunts and rocks of those residents of Cicero who felt outraged by the invasion of their home area. (Some time later a march into all-white residential areas in Milwaukee was led by Father Groppi.)

The wisdom of the Cicero demonstration will, no doubt, be debated for a long time. It was clearly different from the Selma March and Dr. King's other demonstrations. In the earlier efforts the target was an organized body and a body that had both power and authority to comply with the demand that was being made. Suburban neighborhoods, by contrast, are not well organized, and there was no one act by which they could signify compliance with what was being asked. In suggesting that Dr. King selected a poor target, we are not trying to make a sly comparison of King with Gandhi. Gandhi himself was, to a large extent, nonplussed by the diffuse and poorly organized antagonism between Hindu and Moslem neighbors. His decisions on the use of soul-force in this area lacked the brilliant appropriateness of the decisions that had been made in dealing with the well-organized British Colonial Office.

In order to judge the wisdom of Martin Luther King's neighborhood *Satyagraha* alternative targets would have to be considered. One of the most obvious alternatives is the federal Congress, the major distributor of tax funds in the United States. It is significant that in the last months of his career Dr. King did choose this target. Of course, by the time the Poor People's March on Washington had begun, Dr. King was dead, and the new March leadership seemed incapable of pinpointing their demands. The timing was such that they could not hit at one of the key institutional obstacles to a full-scale use of federal revenues for the benefit of slum dwellers. (We refer to the Congressional Seniority system which, together with one-Party dominance of southern districts, keeps superannuated segregationists in the most important Congressional Committee chairmanships. That roadblock could be removed only during the opening days of a session of Congress.)

Dr. King's difficulty in finding a suitable target will be experienced by anyone who realizes that the educational inequities suffered by American children are not going to be corrected by a single act that is within the control of a monolithic opponent. The problem is not a lack of targets but the difficulty of selecting a target that is *capable* of visible *response* to the aspirations of a large and unevenly perceptive constituency.

Mentioning the aspirations relating to education brings us to the topic which, for Gandhi, was of prime importance, viz., the purpose of education. Gandhi kept reiterating his conviction that the primary purpose of education should be the moral and spiritual development of the child. On the surface, at least, American reformers have been less concerned about moral education than about vocational competence. Indeed, the most persistently expressed goal has been the equalization of opportunities *to qualify for preferred employment* in a fast-moving economy. This is clearly the thinking of the two hundred leading businessmen and educators in the Committee for Economic Development; their annual reports have emphasized the economy's need for skilled manpower and the poor man's desire for steady employment. They reject any suggestion that standards be lowered in order to assimilate the "hard core of unemployables."[5] Rather the CED (and, probably, most of the country's educators) are looking for ways to remedy the deficiencies of slum children and bring their performance up to Industry's requirements by:

Headstart programs (preparatory work with preschool children).

Foster homes for abandoned children and for children from broken homes.

Redevelopment programs to replace slums with decent housing and adequate public services.

Birth control programs to prevent families of uneconomic size.

Tutoring and other special aids for culturally deprived children.

Busing of children from poor neighborhoods to schools in more privileged neighborhoods.

Longer probation periods in higher education for students who have difficulties due to inadequate preparatory work.

Special job training programs in government agencies and in industry, programs that not only tolerate the lack of basic skills but also deficiencies in health and habits of living.[6]

The aim of equalizing opportunities *for employment* is predicated upon a belief that the world's economies are being transformed and that participation in productive work is more and more limited to those who have had a good deal of schooling. This same belief has dominated the thinking of publicists who were asked to do something about "depressed economic areas" and "backward countries." Gifts and loans of capital would do these regions no good unless the education of the populace were upgraded.[7]

Community Development and Separatism

Obliquely opposed to this economic orientation of education, but in most cases not quite on Gandhi's beam, have been an odd assortment of Americans who saw the educational needs of disadvantaged people in other terms. The late Professor Baker Brownell was one of the more eloquent spokesmen for these dissenters. Brownell had not accepted as inevitable the urbanization and large-scale industrialization of the human race. When he compared life in factory towns with life in rural communities, the factory towns looked barren. He felt that rural regions could be saved from decadence, even though they had lost some of their former economic importance. In Montana and in Southern Illinois he undertook to prove that a community development program could equip neighbors with organizational skills and attitudes that would enable them to sustain a good life, even though they were not at the centers of industrial and political power.[8]

Brownell's plea was for an education to revive or create intelligent community spirit. He even objected to sending students far away from home for their collegiate studies; that cut off their social roots and, he thought, sapped them of the best kind of motivation.

Brownell's less economic and more "spiritual" conception of education has been supported from some rather surprising quarters. Not a few of the Technical Assistance advisers who had been sent to underdeveloped countries have concluded that industrial evolution was being stopped by a cultural incapacity for cooperation. Two of the frankest statements to this effect are Edward Banfield's *The Moral Basis of a Backward Society* and his *Government Project*.[9] In the first book Banfield marvels at what he calls the amoral familism of a southern Italian community, where it never occurred to the leading citizens to get together and send a delegation to the government to try to secure good roads. In the second book he reported the human cussedness that wrecked a million-dollar project for indigent farm families in Arizona.

Unwelcome support from Brownell's point of view has also come from spokesmen for the more militant Blacks in recent years. They have insisted that the image of Negro inferiority is so pervasive in American culture that the usual means of equalizing educational opportunities will fail. They reject the idea of fitting their children into the dominant industrial society and call for a kind of separatism. The disadvantaged children will continue to drop out of school, they say, until "black is beautiful" and black children have both pride and self-respect.[10] Although some of this talk can be discounted as Marxist demagoguery, it is difficult to believe that the morale problem will disappear as soon as everyone has an opportunity to graduate into a well-paying job.

The limited but real response in disadvantaged neighbor-

75

hoods to Black separatism looks like a crazy about-face, a self-defeating reversal of efforts to escape serfdom and achieve integration. The craziness does not seem so crazy after we read the autobiographical statements of bright Negro children who have won prizes in the School-Profession-Industry-Big Government race track, for example, the following:

Can I destroy in a moment sixteen years of hatred? Is it as great here as I think? I have nothing against the guys at Yale Summer High School, but I constantly wonder if prejudice doesn't linger behind some surreptitious face. I find it almost inconceivable that two places could be so different—one a hell-port of sore spots, the other a Utopia. Then, too, I wonder if here is really Utopia. Do I value the things I have here only because I have been deprived of them for so long at home down South?[11]

For people who have not had the experience of being Jim-Crowed such questionings are almost incomprehensible. In order to take them seriously we would have to imagine ourselves in utterly different circumstances. How would we feel, for example, if the Nazis had won World War II and, after decades of abuse we were admitted to a School for Gauleiters? Would not our morale be shaky? Would we not be afflicted by indecision, lacking confidence in the prospects that were offered to us? If these considerations seem farfetched, it may be well to recall the lengths to which Gandhi went in his educational plans to bolster the self-confidence of the Indian peasant child.

The 1968 New York City teachers' strike and the concurrent trouble at San Francisco State College highlighted a difference in values between the equal-opportunity-in-industry point of view and the community-morale point of view. Both disputes involved an insistence on the part of Black militants that disadvantaged black children needed to be taught by black teachers and furthermore, that they needed enthusiastic instruction in Negro history. No doubt, Baker Brownell would have regarded these demands as perverse and mistaken expressions of the community development point of view. But what other interpretation would an outcast group give to Brownell's fear of what he called "big organizational concepts?" Brownell denied that there is a communal life in large-scale organizations. They miss, he insisted,

> the concrete intimacy in the lives of human beings that Gandhi, for example, always maintained. They have no base, as his thinking always had, the soils and salt, the spinning and the cotton patches, the village schools, gardens and the little communities of men living rather fully with one another.[12]

Brownell's glorification of the small community was challenged by Professor Henry Nelson Wieman. Wieman said that,

> people in such a community often live like turtles, each sticking out his head to attend to matters only when they happen to fall within the narrow bounds of accepted concern. The great city has not only developed a mighty technology, it has broken the shell that narrows human interest.[13]

Brownell retorted that the turtle image applied to urban people as much as to rural people and that only in the decentralized community was there the possibility of communal life.

The Brownell-Wieman exchange warns us that age-old intellectual biases may becloud our judgment of what is needed most by disadvantaged children. Almost since the dawn of history intellectuals have disagreed concerning the benefits of large-scale organization. From the time of Heraclitus and Plato there have been men who would agree with Brownell that individuals get lost in big empires and are easily subjected "to the whims from every quarter and to despotisms by every manipulator of power." But there have also been apologists for the cosmopolitan world that liberates individuals and gives scope to their abilities. Indeed, Brownell's onetime colleague,

Buckminster Fuller, has insisted that the only hope of a good life for all lies in world-wide designs that will bring to full utilization the earth's natural resources.[14] Reforming the environment, he believes, will be easier than reforming people.

From this industrial technology viewpoint the children in deprived communities cannot be given an effective morale-building community experience unless the now-poverty-stricken communities receive aid from the earnings of fabulously productive, large-scale industry. And, it may be pointed out, that the Area Services Division of the University (which Brownell helped to inspire) has steadily drifted away from pep talks and rallies to the supplying of specialized aid in securing grants, contracts and various public services from big government and big industry.

Could Industrialization Be Gandhian?

But did not Brownell claim the authority of Gandhi for his small community idea? Yes, but Gandhi's quarrel was not with big, mechanized industry per se. He objected to the exploitation of men in big industries, to industries that robbed men of their capacity for conscientious behavior, to industries that made men dependent.[15]

The importance of the morale problem is underlined in the testimony of Gandhi's associates. Nehru, speaking in Chicago, put it this way:

> May I tell you of one lesson which helped us tremendously in India in the early days of our struggle? In those days we were weak and had a powerful empire governing us. The great question was: "How can we oppose it?" If anybody raised his head it was struck down. Then Gandhi came and told us not to be afraid. It is a very simple thing to say, but there was something in his voice, in his eyes, and in the way he said these things that had a powerful effect. It is an extraordinary thing how that sense of fear vanished from the Indian people, because they realized what could happen to them.

We, who have been schooled in the pragmatic, scientific technology of the American "techno-structure," are inclined to discount the alleged influence of Gandhi's charisma. We know that there were some other charismatic personalities in the Indian independence movement. We are apt to attribute Gandhi's morale-building power to the fact that he had hit upon some programs of action that were feasible. He called the signals for plays that were within the capabilities of ordinary human beings. Yet, however we explain Gandhi's influence, the historical fact remains that he did something to change the morale of the independence movement.

Precisely what is going on in this discussion? Is it a professorial backing and filling that will come to rest on some dead center? We hope not. We began by asking what could be done to correct the inequalities in educational opportunities. Our question was not concerned with what each of us could do to help some individual child, but what should be the goals of an organized attack upon the problem. It then appeared that the easiest targets are discriminatory laws and institutional policies. The removal of legal discrimination does not equalize opportunities, however, when there exists massive poverty, widespread race prejudice and *de facto* segregation. To combat these obstacles some people favor campaigns for more generous fiscal policies, whereas other people favor campaigns that would satisfy needs for morale building in the disadvantaged groups. This division seems to bring into play some ancient preconceptions. And so, the judgment of suitable strategies has some components that should be empirical findings of fact, whereas they tend to be preconceptions.

It is quite possible that there is no one panacea for the victims of racial discrimination, just as there is no one panacea for physically and emotionally handicapped children. Some, by special educational assistance, may be fitted for life in the big time. Some may only hope for work in a sheltered (subsidized or protected) small community. Some may have to be excused from any kind of productive work. Yet, the utilization of dissatisfaction in the disadvantaged groups and sympathy among

the bystanders can only occur, if there is a measure of agreement on the priority to be assigned to goals of political action.[16]
The priorities deserve our best deliberation; but that does not
imply that our deliberations will take place under conditions
conducive to cool reflection.

We hear the noisy contentions of rival factions. One group
calls for massive appropriations for better schools. Another
has a plan for employing the unskilled. We hear that all urgent
needs cannot be met unless the war and defense budget is cut.
Is that the crucial issue? Or should the first order of business
be curriculum reform, or busing, or something else? Public
attention cannot be concentrated on all causes at once. A choice
must be made.

If any American teacher or student wishes to pay his respects
to the memory of Gandhi, here is a subject to which he may
make a contribution. A bold, Gandhian imagination is needed
to identify next steps for better schooling. What attainable
objectives will satisfy the apparently incompatible requirements? One set of requirements deals with the economic facts
of life: A larger part of the now-disadvantaged minorities need
many skills and attitudes that will give them places and pay-
checks in a sophisticated, technological economy. The other set
of requirements deals with problems resulting from a cruel,
brow-beating history: Both the disadvantaged minorities and
the more privileged segments of society need experiences that
will neutralize (and, possibly, obliterate) the subservient, hang-
dog image that keeps disadvantaged children in an overawed
dither when they compete for the prizes of large-scale organizations.

At this writing rival leaders are formulating programs of
action and inventing slogans that satisfy either the economic
requirement or the morale requirement. To the extent that they
succeed in whipping up popular support, the Image-Changers
counteract the efforts of the Economic-Facts-of-Life Educators,
and vice versa.

Can these apparently contradictory requirements be put into
a computer that will select a unifying program of action? Or

will the resolution come, in the way that Bergson thought all creative next steps come, in the mystical insights of a dedicated man, a man who does not think mechanically, perhaps, a man like Gandhi?

7

The Educational Response
to Social Conflict: Doctrine

THE SETTLEMENT of the Educational Inequality controversy will
not come without social conflict. Like many other public issues,
it has stirred up factions, each faction seeking to impose its will
upon the others. If teachers and students concern themselves
with such public controversies, they can expect opposition,
perhaps even illegal obstruction. They will then have to decide
whether to fight or to shut up. If they choose to fight, will
Gandhi's *Satyagraha* offer them a desirable alternative to riot
and mayhem?

For the tenured and tonsured members of our educational
monasteries *Satya (Truth)* is a sacred object. This makes for a
built-in receptiveness to Gandhism, although the receptiveness
is reduced by a time-honored desire to rise above the partisanship of ordinary politics. Official thinkers have held out the
hope that the discovery and dissemination of true knowledge
would somehow bring public blessings without involving our
schools and colleges in unseemly brawls. The force in *Satyagraha* would, they supposed, be applied by the alumni rather
than by the faculty and present student body.

Now that many educational institutions have been cata-
pulted, willy-nilly, into raging political battles, many of us are
taking a more serious interest in Gandhi's claim that it is possible to engage in political contests without a resort to violence.

Regardless of previous disclaimers of partisan intent, our schools have been forced to take controversial positions regarding the violence that erupted on campus. We used to think we could choose between partisanship and nonpartisanship. Now the schools seem to be unavoidably partisan, and the choice is between violent and nonviolent partisanship.

American Efforts to Reduce Violence

Up to a certain point, it may be contended, a major part of the educational establishment has for a long time given instruction in the arts of nonviolence. Although, as we shall concede, the American schoolmen's advocacy of nonviolence fell short of Gandhi's commitments, a quick review of this side of American education will not be out of place. From kindergarten to professional school the reduction of violence has been accepted as one of the fruits of enlightenment. Enlightenment has not usually been conceived, as Gandhi conceived it, as a kind of self-purification, albeit that point of view is occasionally in evidence. The more common opinion, however, holds that violence is a wasteful and ineffective means of resolving conflicts and should be replaced by more intelligent methods in every sphere of life. The idea is that "knowledge is power," not only power over nature but also power over human nature; the teachers and scientists, accordingly, search for the causes of violence and for new techniques for removing those causes. Illustrations are readily at hand in pedagogy, in psychiatry, in business and public administration, and in the fields of law and criminology.

In the elementary and secondary schools (and in the teacher training institutions), for example, the orthodox view of "discipline" problems is that they are symptoms of unmet needs. Instead of resorting to counter-violence (caning, etc.) teachers should look for and control whatever it is that makes boys "bad." Perhaps, the curriculum is outmoded or the teaching methods are unnecessarily irritating. Perhaps, there is a medical or a psychiatric problem that needs expert attention. In any case, tantrums are not to be met with counter-tantrums; vandalism and quarreling are to be stopped by something better directed than a mere display of superior force. Although this "philosophy of education" has been put to a severe test in the recent years of urban turbulence, nonviolence is still the pedagogue's ideal. Even if he teaches in a "blackboard jungle," he may refuse to return to the old break-the-child's-will discipline, explaining the ineffectiveness of his own nonviolent methods by saying that the intelligent remedy calls for resources greater than his own.

Pretty much the same story can be told concerning a number of university-level disciplines that address themselves to other problems of violent behavior. Many of the changes in psychology, medicine, psychiatry, and the administrative arts are regarded as advances because they have been responsible for the virtual disappearance of "violent wards" in mental hospitals, of slave-driving methods in places of work, and industrial warfare in labor relations.[1]

When we turn to educators' attitudes toward crime, the picture is not so consistent. Yet, it must be said that law professors and university criminologists have generally been in the forefront of movements to combat crime with something more effective than sheer counterviolence and severe punishments. Recognizing that much of the personnel of police departments and prisons is not university-trained, a number of universities have offered in-service adult education in an effort to substitute "modern" methods for the sometimes panicky, sometimes irascible use of brute force.[2] There have, of course, been other influences at work, but educators have been conspicuous in the discouragement of "the third degree" (torture in interrogations), gunplay, high-speed chases, ball-and-chain shackling, spread-eagling and the like.

In pedagogy, psychiatry, the administration arts, and law, American teachers and students have been advocating what the police work experts call the concept of "minimum force." As the matter is expressed in the FBI Manual, "use only the minimum force necessary to control the situation." The idea rests upon a faith that intelligent problem-solving (Professor John Dewey's phrase) will invent techniques that are more effective than impassioned violence and restraint in preventing undesirable behavior.

Ends and Means

Professor Dewey, whose "Instrumentalist," problem-solving philosophy has been influential, repeatedly talked about "ends and means" in a way that sounded very much like Gandhi's discourses on the same theme. Indeed, Mrs. Joan Bondurant in her study, *The Conquest of Violence*, assumed that Dewey and Gandhi were in agreement up to a certain point, Dewey merely stopping short of one step that Gandhi took.[3] Mrs. Bondurant, unfortunately, overlooked a fundamental difference between the two philosophies, an oversight that has obscured the whole subject.

It is true that Dewey insisted that means and ends are inseparable parts of the same situation. When, during the 1930s, the Marxists invited Dewey to join them in rescuing America from a terrible economic crisis by revolutionary tactics, Dewey said that the Communists could not bring about a democratic, warless society by a "dictatorship of the proletariat."[4] But Dewey's objection to dictatorship did not rest upon an assumption that certain means are intrinsically evil. Dewey rejected the theory of moral absolutes. He denied that "the end justifies the means" because he believed that life has more than one end (more than one good). He was willing to say that the ends, *all* of the ends considered together, justify the means.[5] Dewey rejected violence as a means, in many cases, because—among the ends or consequences—there would be the establishment of the habit of using violence and there would fail to be a cultivation of the habits and arts of intelligent discussion and negotiation.

Dewey's preference for nonviolent methods and Gandhi's nonviolence were poles apart. Gandhi sounded like Dewey when he argued for a means-ends continuum, but there was a non-Deweyan idea in Gandhi's comparison of means to the roots of a tree and ends, to the leaves and fruit. Some roots, Gandhi believed, were absolutely immoral, whereas, for Dewey nothing should be judged to be inherently bad. Such judgments, according to Dewey, should always be based upon knowledge of the consequences.

Summing up the last few pages, we conclude that American educators readily join with Gandhi in efforts to *reduce* violence. At the same time, most of them, howevermuch they talk about human beings as ends in themselves, approach the subject as a technical problem. Few of them recognize in violence an absolute and intrinsic evil.

The Passive Resisters and the Nullificationists

We turn, now, to another partial agreement between many American school men and Gandhi, viz., regarding nonviolent civil disobedience as an alternative to violence. A number of American pacifists have documented the indubitable fact that passive resistance and (to a lesser extent) active civil disobedience have American and European origins that are independent of Indian and, particularly, Gandhian inspiration. The documentation of this thesis, for example, by Professor Staughton Lynd in his *Nonviolence in America*,[6] systematically neglects the American use of civil disobedience in causes that pacifists regard as evil. We refer to the nullification tradition. Among the nullifiers were the colonists who collectively and conscientiously disobeyed the Orders in Council prior to American independence, the slave owners who defied the federal government in the 1830s (without a resort to arms), the drinkers who were "scofflaws" during the Prohibition era, and the local communities that would not accept "dictation" from Washington or their state capitol. Representative of the last-named nullification was "The Battle of Blue Earth County," the record of a Minnesota county's defiance of the federal government in the administration of Old Age Assistance and Aid to Dependent Children.[7] Also in the nullification tradition are the business interests and the southern communities that engage in apparently hopeless litigation, avowedly trying to have a statute declared unconstitutional but actually intent on wearing down the enforcement agency and eroding the public support for enforcement.

The effect of the pacifists' systematic bias in selecting historical precedents is to obscure profound differences between American and Gandhian civil disobedience. It is true that the Quakers, the Mennonites, some of the Transcendentalists and a few of the American Anarchists were, at times, quite close to Gandhi's religious and moral motivations. But these little minorities are overshadowed by instruction given by American schools in what we have called the "nullification" form of civil disobedience.

Resulting Views of Civil Disobedience

The graduates of our multipurpose, decentralized educational system do not all receive the same indoctrination; but it can safely be asserted that many of them come out with a more or less clear idea of civil disobedience. Civil disobedience is defined as a form of political action, vaguely located somewhere between lawful protest and revolution. It is a set of techniques. Some of the techniques are permissible and may even be necessary for the health of a free society. The most certainly allowable form of civil disobedience occurs when someone wishes to test the legality of an executive order, the judgment of a prosecutor or the constitutionality of a statute.

Civil disobedience can be undertaken by men with any sort of motivation: moral scruple, religious conviction, self-interest, or seditious intent. Disobedience is a form of bargaining, making use of bargaining power that is not ordinarily brought into play. Its effectiveness lies in its "nuisance value." Nuisance value may be tolerated, as long as certain services vital to the community or the nation are not threatened.

Most Americans have learned in school that civil disobedience sometimes is successful in changing the law and in those cases it is usually "a good thing." Labor unions, for instance, won the right to bargain and to strike by defying court orders that branded them as illegal conspiracies. But when the United Auto Workers attempted "sit-down" strikes in 1937, they were "going too far," and that kind of disobedience was stopped. Similarly, the members of pacifist churches won exemption from combat duty by disobedience to orders; but, it is widely held, the recent draft card burners have "gone too far."

Many Americans were surprised when the Negroes of Montgomery, Alabama, engaged in a year-long boycott of the city bus line and when, somewhat later, Florida students began conducting "sit-ins" at segregated restaurants and lunch counters. They were surprised that southern Negroes engaged in these tactics, but the tactics themselves were no surprise. The various forms of civil disobedience were understood as tactics, *pragmatically* chosen by the disobedient and *pragmatically* allowed or prohibited by the authorities and the by-standing public.

It seems fairly certain that, when the Rev. Martin Luther King began his advocacy of civil disobedience, his most stubborn difficulty was infusing the disobedience with love of the enemy, a Christian and Gandhian freedom from hatred. Especially after he began organizing colored people in the northern cities, he was in a "two-front-war." Facing him were the segregationists and discriminators. On his flanks, however, were leaders like Saul Alinsky and Stokely Carmichael, appealing to the disadvantaged to use their "nuisance value" to force concessions, without love and without theological conviction.

Alinsky had set up his Industrial Areas Foundation as a kind of service bureau for poor people, and since the 1940s had promised to give poor neighborhoods the knowhow of the labor movement. Alinsky frankly encouraged the expression of bitter resentment, once saying that it was necessary to "rub raw the sores of discontent."[8]

Carmichael, getting his start in the sixties in the Student *Non-violent* Co-ordinating Committee, moved rapidly toward an emphasis on power and away from King's dream of an integrated community. Although Carmichael's book, *Black Power*, retained the hope of nonviolent social change, his speeches and statements to the press were full of animosity and gave encouragement not only to separatists but also to those who were seeking revenge. Carmichael's phrase "black power" caught on overnight, and by the time of Dr. King's assassination even conservative Negro leaders were talking about "Blacks" instead of Negroes."[9]

The sort of obstructionism advocated by Alinsky and Carmichael was purely tactical; it was not moored in theology and it was not restricted to men who had the discipline of moral good will in the Gandhian sense. As such, it was within what we call the Madisonian tradition of American politics. Carmichael, of course, soon jeopardized his legitimacy within the Madisonian tradition, when he sought aid and comfort from Fidel Castro and other sworn enemies of the United States, but his "deviation" was not in substituting hatred for love; his deviation was in going beyond the American limits of "permissible" civil disobedience.

All of this has to be said and much more besides, in order to understand what Americans have learned in school about civil disobedience. With notable exceptions, their teachers have acquainted them with civil disobedience, as they have also acquainted them with nonviolence, as *techniques* to be used and judged prudentially. The little sects that did practice nonviolent passive resistance as an integral part of their way of life have been treated as curiosities, respected for the nobility of their ideals, but not taken seriously as models for dealing with the great controversial issues of today.

One indication of the superficiality of resemblances between typical American thinking about nonviolent civil disobedience and the Gandhian teaching is the neglect of the latter in social science treatises. It is true that a number of American social scientists and historians have addressed themselves to studies of Gandhi. When, however, they undertake general theorizing about political conflict in their own discipline, their "foreign" references are usually to Europeans. For example, a symposium in *The Annals* of the American Academy of Political and Social Science, entitled "Patterns of Violence," contained no comment on Gandhi and only a brief comment on Dr. King.[10]

The difficulty that American educators experience in going all the way with Gandhi on nonviolence and conscientious civil disobedience is not easily explained. Perhaps it is that they have accepted a large-scale, multipurpose, pluralistic society. Although they continue to talk about big cities and nations as communities, they really do not see these political entities as communities. Cities and nations are conveniences for avoiding some common evils, but there is not much that can rightfully be called a common good. The conflicts of interests are innumerable, and political intelligence is needed to work out a viable adjustment of the opposed pressure groups that represent these divergent interests.

In such a world there is a reason for courtesy and good faith, but there is little hope that strangers will cease being strangers or that they will stop bargaining at arm's length. It is in (nearly) everyone's interest to avoid destructive warfare, but no one can be expected to act as if the whole world were one community.

If this pluralistic pressure-group picture is the dominant doctrine among American educators, their preference for a prudential approach to conflict is understandable. They want to reduce violence, but they do not have Gandhi's orientation for the ideal of absolute nonviolence. They can see the need for occasional civil disobedience as a safety valve or as a means of keeping institutions responsive to changing pressures. But they interpret disobedience as the weapon of otherwise weak bargainers who—as a last resort—use their own nuisance value. And they do not understand how the love of opponents and the need for self-suffering can be more than propaganda, at least, when practiced on a large scale. Something like this is the doctrine with which our schools approach the problems of social conflict.

8

Confrontation

THE GANDHI Centennial catches American teachers and students at a moment when they may be in a mood to reconsider their opinions about the relation of education to social conflict. They may be ready to give more than a polite gesture in the direction of Gandhian love and self-sacrifice. Many a campus is the scene of student strikes and many a high school has been plagued by knifings, vandalism and riots. This is unprecedented in the history of the United States. Until 1966 we had a rather smug complacency as we compared our own orderly processes with the strike-bound schools in Latin America and other less favored regions. Now we have confrontations as disturbing and as puzzling as those we used to view from afar.

During the past three years there have been many investigations of student unrest. Not a few of these investigations have been conducted by well-known experts, employing research techniques that had previously cleared up difficulties in other parts of our society. The techniques are, for the most part, empirical or "behavioral" and they are analytical. We shall review their findings in a sketchy way, adequately enough, we hope, to show that the inquiries have the orientation outlined in the preceding chapter. That is an orientation in a pluralistic, noncommunal world, with trouble spots being interpreted as definable, unsatisfied interests.

The investigators have tried to identify a) the kind of students whose grievances led to the trouble, b) precisely what triggered the violence, and *c)* what reforms might conceivably prevent a recurrence.

Analysis of Student Dissidents

The trouble-generating student grievances appear not to have been uniform. At Brooklyn College the disturbance of October 19, 1967, started as a result of the activities of students opposed to the Viet Nam War. At San Francisco State College the disorders of October and November, 1968, were traced to the agitation of Black militants. The same was the case at Northwestern University in the spring of 1968. The biggest explosions (at the University of California at Berkeley and Columbia University) involved both war protesters and Black militants, but there was also dissatisfaction with the internal policies of the universities. The grievances concerning university life have been sorted out as *1)* complaints about the irrelevance of instruction and research to contemporary social problems; *2)* bureaucratic ineptitude and injustice in the services and disciplinary actions affecting students; and *3)* undue pressure for academic performance.[1]

In nearly every instance, a relatively small part of the teaching staff, usually junior faculty members, have been identified as sympathizers or instigators. At Columbia University, and at several other places, where the administrative response to the initial difficulties was very clumsy, faculty sentiment swung over to the side of the dissident students, at least, for a while. The principal characters in the confrontations, however, were a minority of students on one side and administrative officers on the other.

Nearly all of the investigations have asked, what was the mood and what was the thinking of the students who blocked traffic, attacked other students, seized administrative offices, stopped classwork, and otherwise disrupted the order of the schools? The answer to this question is that the mood was generally one of frustration and hopelessness, regardless of the nature of the grievance. This mood was most articulate in the case of the "New Left", young people who wanted to do something to stop the Viet Nam War. They wanted the universities to discontinue cooperating with draft boards, military recruiters, and Defense Department research; they also wanted radical measures to right racial injustices; and, to both ends, they were supporting maverick candidates for public office.

Dr. Clark Kerr (ex-President of the University of California) thought the staff of the *Harvard Crimson* had expressed a widespread feeling, when they told him that,

> they seemed to be a generation which was condemned either to be ignored (when it went through channels and obeyed the law and did the right things procedurally), or to get attention by going outside the law but with negative consequences. They said: We are a generation condemned to no influence or to a negative influence at a time when we so deeply want to have a positive influence.[2]

Tom Hayden, prominent among the "New Left" spokesmen, put it this way:

> The American way of life is a closed door, or rather a slammed door. Idealistic people—youth, students, minority groups—are not allowed to enter, not permitted expressions of self-determination. For them, there is no other real alternative except to go into a movement to try to open up a life based on more worthy values. The task is to create more Chicagos in our cities, more Columbias on our campuses—and not be good Germans by accepting the system as it is.[3]

Typical of the "New Left" line was an article, "The Student as Nigger," by Jerry Farber:

> Back in kindergarten, you found out that teachers only love children who stand in nice straight lines and that's where it's been at ever since. Nothing changes except to get worse. What school amounts to, for white and black kids

alike, is a 12-year course in how to be slaves. What else could explain what I see in a freshman class? They've got the slave mentality: obliging and ingratiating on the surface, but hostile and resentful underneath.[4]

This lack of faith in established institutions has been generalized by faculty sympathizers (like Professors Noam Chomsky and Herbert Marcuse) into an assertion of the futility of all normal and accepted forms of protest. Chomsky called for what he labelled as the "de-Nazification" of the United States.[5]

Quotations from the New Left are conspicuous in many reports, mainly because they are more available and more eloquent than the comments of other dissident elements. A similar hopelessness, however, seems to characterize the Black militants and the "non-political" students whose gripes have concerned rules relating to instruction, automobiles, drinking, dormitory hours, and student discipline. Most of the rebels dismiss the usual "Student Government" as a time-wasting joke. Ordinarily concerned with trivia, student governments— they say—get the "run-around" whenever they propose that something be done about poor teaching or about the unjust decisions of third-layer bureaucrats.[6]

The Black militants, of course, are drawn from a segment of society only recently present in large numbers in the big schools. In their background is an experience that is relatively unknown to white students, viz. experience with discriminatory justice. As Professor Cornelius Golightly has noted,

> Among Negroes, law-abiding and non-law-abiding, educated and uneducated, there is a deep psychological and philosophical repudiation of the white man's law. Even where prudence effects a careful obedience to the letter of the law there is little philosophical respect for the law.[7]

Analysis of Institutional Failures

When the investigators turn to the institutional failures, the diagnosis is largely in terms that teachers have used in explaining and prescribing for the disorders in noneducational institutions. Explanatory principles that have previously been applied to factories, hospitals, prisons and offices seem not to have been taken seriously in the teaching and research organizations that helped to work out the principles. It is an ironic situation, which may remind us of the farmer who told the farm adviser: "Don't give me any more advice; I'm not farming half as good as I know how now."

The Cox Commission, for example, took notice of the lack of channels of communication at Columbia University. It was only after students had seized the university buildings that efforts were made to establish some *ad hoc* grievance procedures. And in other schools, where such procedures existed on paper, they did not work. Students, who demanded reversal of a decision or some change in the rules, discovered that they needed a full-time staff of legal and academic experts. Secondary schools could act on many matters only by the concurrence of a large number of authorities. Universities had policies that represented the agreement of a vast network, not only within the university, but outside, as well. As Dr. Oliver Caldwell has said:

> The *status quo* in American education is maintained by a delicate balance between literally hundreds of organizations. They range from teachers' associations to accrediting organizations, to groupings of professionals, to councils of learned societies.[8]

Dr. Caldwell could have added to his list: state legislatures, sectional and industrial pressure groups, and various governmental bureaucracies.

Although these complicated arrangements can be viewed as a triumph in democratic, large-scale organization, the democracy is limited to individuals and groups who are expert, specialized and well-organized. For the inexperienced, transient and poorly organized students, the complicated structure of our school system has a very different meaning.

Thus it appears that, in many localities, no one in the administration, in the faculty or in the board of control made sure that the school had effective applications of what the experts were recommending to other institutions to prevent the frustration of the inexpert; viz., ombudsmen, grievance procedures, shop committees, house organs to explain the rules and the policy changes, suggestion boxes, or the polling and interviewing of all concerned.[9]

Two other large-organizational measures were also missing or halfhearted in the schools that had mushroomed from little academies to huge multi-versities. One neglected measure was the provision for fairly small work groups. Industrial and military analysts had long since developed the concept of "span of control." Although they have retreated from simple prescriptions concerning supervision, they continue to insist that the size of the smallest units of organization needs careful study. It is no secret that the morale of combat units depends on identification with the team as much as it does on patriotism; and industrial productivity probably depends less upon company loyalty than upon the *esprit de corps* in the shop or craft unit. But, in the desperate effort to take care of expanding enrollments, many college classes were allowed to become larger and larger; and furthermore, dormitory facilities were assigned in such a way that students could complete four years of coursework and on commencement day still be strangers to everyone they encountered on campus.

The other oft-violated organizational principle was the proposition that large organizations need special processes to provide the "leadership function." It is widely held that industrial enterprises, as they grow in size and complexity, depend less and less upon the personal traits of the men in high office and more and more upon means that are built into the organization for identifying dangers and opportunities and securing adjustment to changes in the environment.[10] We have already noted that lack of polling and interviewing in the regular operation of many educational institutions. What is worse, from the standpoint of large-organization theory, is the fact that faculty and trustee control of our largest educational institutions is the same as it was in the days of small schools. It is as if an act of Congress were required every time the chlorine dosage needed to be changed in the local waterworks. Or, a more plausible analogy might have it that the board of directors of General Motors, after clearances all the way up the administrative hierarchy, would pass on each change in the body style.

Another way of identifying the organizational trouble of the schools is to notice how they stimulated interest in public affairs without providing adequate opportunities for acting on such interests (prior to graduation). It is one of the boasts of American educators that they provide civic instruction for children and young people. This involves not only an acquaintance with conditions that need to be corrected, but also exhortations to participate in efforts at the correction. These exhortations frequently take the form of "viewing with alarm."[11] Yet, the immediate outlet for an aroused interest is, for most students, writing a paper. The professor, at least, *does* something when he delivers a lecture. He can say, "See what I did!" But when can the student say, "See what I did!"? There are, of course, some exceptions: Peace Corps, Vista Corps, work-study programs, the Citizenship Clearing House, and (in the sciences) professor-and-student research projects. But, for the great majority of students, there was nothing of the sort.

Alienation

Instruction at the university level includes some studies that are not in the spirit of pragmatic technology. They bring acquaintance with the writings of poets, philosophers and revolutionists, who have articulated a mood of frustration in the presence of large-scale organizations. The Jeremiads of Marx, T. S. Eliot, Nietzsche, Brunner, Sartre and Marcuse provide phrases for the angry young men; while playwrights and novelists make plausible the sickness of the world. If we had to select one extreme contrast to the technical view of social conflict (outlined in the preceding chapter), we would choose

Kafka's *The Trial*. That disturbing story has now been read by several generations of college students. It depicts an inexpressably hopeless situation: a poor creature, caught in the toils of the law and standing trial. The miserable defendant never succeeds in learning with what crime he is charged; he never understands what is happening. This absurd predicament appeals to young people whose plans for marriage and career are unpredictably blasted by draft boards and a war whose purpose is never clear. It appeals to naked and solitary individuals who are being lectured on the corporate world that manipulates "us," but which "we" never seem to be able to control. "We" are victims of "the Establishment." "We" are alienated. "We" are the misfits.

This mood receives confirmation when some hastily organized demonstration is met with "police brutality." And, here, we return to the violation of rules in the "Industrial Management Handbook" (which the colleges of Business Administration have so kindly prepared for large industrial corporations and which the administrative officers and instructional staffs of some universities have not taken personally). Security and discipline are in some schools entrusted to inadequately trained and poorly supervised junior officers. In the early stages of the trouble at Berkeley and at Brooklyn, for example, crucial decisions were made by assistant deans of students. At Columbia the occupied buildings were finally cleared by policemen who had had no special training for dealing with students, and the same lack of special training was evident in Chicago, when students were demonstrating in the vicinity of the Democratic National Convention. (In these and other cases, the police were infuriated by clever taunts and ingenious unconventionality.)

Summing up this picture from one point of view, we can say that it is a picture of information and techniques half used, of principles spasmodically applied. The hell-raising students are keenly aware of imperfections in the university and its environment; but they act like greenhorns (or cynical revolutionists) when they attempt to negotiate with "the power structure." The paid officers and employees of the schools are busily engaged in solving a host of difficult problems but, when unrest appears among the students, the complicated machinery appears to be paralyzed and nearly everyone is "letting George do it." This characterization, happily, does not fit all public school systems and universities; but it does fit those that have made the newspaper headlines and are, therefore, accepted as representative of "the crisis of our age."

Could a Gandhi Solve Our Unsolved Problem?

The American university's explosive conflicts in the sixties rattle a skeleton in the closet of Occidental philosophy. They bring up what William James called "the dilemma of determinism." And on this topic no one, from Locke and Spinoza to Sartre and Gilbert Ryle, seems to make much sense.

There is an "intellectualist" tradition, going straight back to the Greeks, which dismisses as a "false problem" any suggestion that men are ever faced with questions to which there is no answer "but the dumb turning of the will as we say, 'I will even have it so.' "[12] The intellectualists are holding to their assumption, so important as the faith of scientists, that nothing is unintelligible. If everything can be understood, how can there be any real uncertainty, any ultimate "freedom of the will"?

Opposed to intellectualism are a long line of voluntarists who have started from the common sense view of human action but somehow ended up with wild, incredible assertions of responsibility for nearly everything in the universe. This tradition goes back to the ancient Hebrews, reinforced along the way by the moral promptings of countless tribesmen.

Anglo-American philosophical journals have, during the past decade, published much on "the language of thought and the language of action," the relation of description to prescription, and the like. On the continent of Europe the presses have turned out ponderous tomes on the subject of guilt, anxiety, "the voluntary and the involuntary," "on being oneself," and the like. Possibly, there are some new approaches to the puzzles about theory and practice; possibly, a new approach will yield an improvement on the formulas of the classical western philosophers. As of now, the improvements, if any, are not very obvious.

Why not see whether Gandhi's example may be helpful to students, teachers and administrators who are so good at describing and explaining what is going on but—with reference to some of their present disagreements—seem to be unable to act, unable to apply some of their own theories?

Consider the following "thought experiment," prompted by a reader's inquiry. A reader of Gandhi's paper had asked if violence might not sometimes be a proper means, say, to drive a thief out of his house. Gandhi replied that there was no question about the effectiveness of violence in securing such a result as driving out the thief, but he added:

> It is perfectly true that (the English) used brute force and that it is possible for us to do likewise, but by using similar means we can get only the same thing that they got. You will admit that we do not want that.

Then, turning to the question of the thief, Gandhi asked what the reader would suggest, if the thief happened to be his own father. Would he advise the same recourse to violence regardless of whether the thief was a white man or an Indian? And what would be the reader's state of mind after he resorted to brute force, especially if he failed to drive the thief out. Why not, at a suitable opportunity, attempt to reason with the thief?

> Instead of being angry with him, take pity on him. You think that this stealing habit must be a disease with him. Henceforth, you, therefore, keep your doors and windows open, you change your sleeping place, and you keep your things in a manner most accessible to him. The robber comes again and is confused as all this is new to him; nevertheless, he takes away your things. But his mind is agitated. He

inquires about you in the village, he comes to learn about your broad and loving heart, he repents, he begs your pardon, and leaves off the stealing habit. He becomes your servant, and you will find for him honourable employment. This is the second method. Thus, you see, different means have brought about totally different results. I do not wish to deduce from this that robbers will act in the above manner or that all will have the same pity and love like you, but I only wish to show that fair means alone can produce fair results, and that, at least in the majority of cases, if not indeed in all, the force of love and pity is infinitely greater than the force of arms. There is harm in the exercise of brute force, never in that of pity.[13]

Gandhi seems to recognize that this fairy tale is far-fetched, but what may be relevant to our predicament is Gandhi's imaginativeness. Confronted by a man whose purposes run counter to his own, Gandhi contemplates a course of action that involves the sacrifice of what he himself wants and that which his wife and family probably regard as indispensable. He is looking for some way to bring a reconciliation between the thief and law-abiding citizens, and he is ready to "do the impossible." You can hear his wife protest: "What, let the thief have my best sari? And our food? What will the children eat tomorrow? And how do you know that the thief will not hurt the children and molest me? Perhaps, he will even kill you!"

What Gandhi has done is to bring into his deliberations a lot of desires and fears that are seldom considered when we "face our problems." He has overcome the "psychological necessities." He has succeeded in doing what the ancient western stoics hoped to do, viz., to loosen the grip of the human desire for comfort, wealth, honor, safety, and freedom. The stoics argued that all of these goods are uncertain, largely not within our power to control; hence, we should not become panicky or hysterical when we lose them or seem likely to lose them.[14]

Whether there can ever be very many stoics is not the point

at issue here. The point is that it is not customary for administrative councils to consider methods of dealing with turbulent students, if the methods involve risk of the administrator's life and limb. It is not customary for faculty councils to give serious thought to a plan that would mean a loss of faculty privileges. It is unusual for a board of control to forget about the budget while debating the kinds of political freedom to be allowed on campus.

We are all sitting behind Maginot Lines. Perhaps, we are all fighting past wars. We try to maintain in the emerging conflicts of today the activities to which we are accustomed, the activities that may have been lifesavers in former battles.

Consider the unthinkability of changing the ways in which we "maintain high standards." Here is a "psychological necessity" that now immobilizes many schools and keeps them from "doing something" about student dissatisfaction. Seventy-five years ago, when there were terribly weak departments in nearly every college, accrediting agencies insisted that all course offerings be approved by an all-college curriculum committee. Now that unaccredited institutions are the exception, retention of this tight central control results in endless delays and an incredible waste of time in committee work. The same is true of the requirement that all "general education" offerings be set up and approved by an all-university committee or council.

Seventy-five years ago, when the quality of high schools and colleges varied from A to Z, accrediting agencies also disciplined institutions that failed to require so many thousand hours of class time for the high school diploma, and about the same number of hours of class time for the bachelor's degree. Today there are many students who should not be required to "serve time" in conformity with this old mechanical standard. Part of their class time would be better spent in reading, tutoring, field work, etc.

Although the more enlightened accrediting agencies have encouraged their members to do some experimenting, these and many other once-rigid requirements have most of the schools in a mental strait jacket. A few of the big universities have been experimenting with small undergraduate colleges. Five hundred to a thousand students are admitted to each college, which is a residential group as well as an academic unit. The college has its own faculty, and the faculty is permitted to make some innovations in the content and methods of instruction without clearances from all of the veto groups in the university. Thus far, the moves in this promising direction have been timid, inhibited by the fears of vested interests and the spectre of prohibitive costs. Undoubtedly, there are difficulties here, but they should be weighed—not against the advantages of what was conventional under conditions in the 1940s or 1950s—but against the disadvantages of the strike-torn schools of today. The confrontations now occurring in the universities (and in the high schools) should be having an unsettling effect upon our habits, even upon habits that are fortified by arguments about "the inconceivability" of having insufficient class time to "cover" our favorite subject.

Administrators and teachers have compulsions about respectability, dignity, economic security, and personal safety. If a college president went on a hunger strike in order to use soul-force on rebellious students, his sanity would be questioned. If a faculty offered probation instead of expulsion to failing students on condition that they report for five hours tutoring per week, and if each professor offered to do that much tutoring, the school would be branded "Flunk-out U."

Students have psychological necessities, too; and some of them stand in the way of intelligent settlements. In view of the fact that we who make these assertions are teachers it may be well to let our student readers decide which of their own supposedly "irresistible" impulses might be resistible. A few of the questionable impulses are:

1. The demand for ousting certain officials instead of trying to change their views. (Can we draw Gandhi's conclusion after studying the history of the French Revolution?)[15]
2. The insistence on a final showdown on all issues at once.[16]
3. The contemptuous rejection of scholarship that has no immediate "relevance" to present-day issues, as now un-

derstood. (Is there some parallel here to what happened in German schools after the Nazi take-over?)[17]

4. The impatience with formality. (Is this an invitation to the rule of naked power whenever agreement cannot be achieved?)

5. The demand for immediate enjoyments. (Is all asceticism really stupid?)

The Idea of Self-Purification

The point of this excursion into academic conventionality is that, under crisis conditions, scoffers may be surprised by their own second thoughts about Gandhi's efforts at "self-purification." If scholarly communities have so very much knowledge that is not now being used in the resolving of campus conflicts, there must be some members of those communities who are prisoners of their own passions. If the common complaint is that we are too powerless or too busy to do what we know needs to be done, is it not possible that some of our time-consuming routines are not really essential?

A Gandhian imagination is needed, no doubt, to perceive the points at which the logjam can be broken. But will that perception come to anyone who does not criticize *himself*?[18] Gandhi may be said to have added to the Christian doctrine ("Love thy neighbor as thyself") another injunction: "Criticize thyself as thy neighbor." His belief in the need for self-purification does not assume that the purified person will abandon partisanship or meekly submit to the opponent's demands. He does, however, assume what Henry Wieman has called a "two-level commitment." It is a commitment to the best partisan cause that one can find at the moment and, alongside that, another commitment to "whatever cause will seem best in the future."[19] This is a commitment to a certain openness, a willingness to change.

Gandhi did not expect the future of mankind to be a miraculous harmony, a society without conflict. He did feel an obligation to work for the best of the various alternative futures that may be within the realm of possibility. Of course, many publicists have shared that outlook. What was remarkable in Gandhi's vision was his escape from a certain one-sidedness in the conception of change.

The usual idea of bargaining is that I make an offer and then you accept or you make a counter-offer. The usual idea of a duel is that you thrust and I parry. The usual idea of legislation is that I propose and you offer an amendment. Gandhi somehow came to realize that he who offers, thrusts or proposes need not be limited by the past and present condition of himself and his adversary. I do not have to make offers that assume the preservation of all my present comforts, interests and inhibitions. If I do that, my action is dependent upon a great many conditions, and what I can propose to my adversary is quite limited. I then wait for my adversary to respond, and my action is thus further dependent and limited. Gandhi somehow acquired a conception of social conflict and change in which the possibilities of action were expanded and less limited. In this liberated conception I thrust, not only at you but also at myself. I make offers, not only to you, but to myself, the self that is bound up with the *status quo*. In this way the negotiation is freed from many of the delays and impasses that are so common in arm's-length bargaining. This emancipation shows itself, not only in the unconventionality of Gandhi's civil disobedience, but also in the choice of a target among established policies. There are limits, of course, to Gandhi's flexibility, and he talks about these limits with the vocabulary of "principles and tactics." It isn't a very helpful vocabulary; but, if we have to use it, we may say that Gandhi opened up new possibilities of tactics by conceiving of tactics against not only a stubborn opponent but also against certain stubborn oppositions within himself, oppositions standing in the way of reconciliation.

Moral Education

We can sum up a Gandhian appraisal of our schools by evaluating the contributions which the schools make to moral education. Gandhi believed that moral standards and commitments are acquired by participation in communal activities. In this belief he agreed with a long line of western educators, from Aristotle to Dewey. What gives Gandhian comments a special relevance for our time is their focus upon the problem of the disadvantaged, the youth whose activities confirm them in habits of dependence rather than initiative, in animal-like selfishness rather than in generosity, in attitudes of violence as a reaction to frustration rather than in some constructive response, such as, *Satyagraha.*

From this standpoint, the preschool and elementary school education of American children is very uneven in quality but, on the whole, deserves a better rating than the educational programs for adolescents. Our high schools and colleges, together with community organizations and employers of part-time workers, provide opportunities for the right sort of action to a sizable *fraction* of the students. But, for the drop-outs and for many who do in a halfhearted way earn their diplomas, schooling in the eight years from age fourteen to age twenty-two means sitting in class five days per week. And, in the sitting position, the students are—most of the time—merely listening. If, outside of school hours, they engage in exciting activities (such as sports, adult-baiting, or adventures with the law), these activities have little connection with the words that they are learning in school.

John Erskine used to say that athletics was the only subject that was well taught in American schools. So far as the moral side of education is concerned, his statement can be defended today. Teamwork, sportsmanship, and courage acquire "more than a verbal meaning" for boys and girls who are habituated by repeated playing of games under rules that are enforced by peer opinion. In the lives of many children there is no comparable "practicum" for the teachings concerning politics and work. Thus it happens that children who have memorized the tolerance slogans of our founding fathers fly into a rage the first time they encounter a really "absurd" opinion. As Hartshorn and May found over forty years ago, children who could repeat the Sunday School lessons about "honesty" and "truth-fulness" were no more honest and truthful in practice than those who had not picked up this verbal learning. And, when it comes to self-respect and self-reliance, there is reason to believe that students who have passed a written examination on Emerson's *Self Reliance* have no better emotional conditioning than the Americans that Pierre Janet used to encounter. (They kept repeating the then-faddish slogan, "Every day in every way I am getting better and better," but Janet said he had never encountered more dejected individuals.)

It can truly be said that many adults have to learn temperance for the first time, when they reach middle age, *after* intemperate habits have broken their health. Others learn tolerance the hard way, after they take on a job that puts them on one side or the other of a labor-management bargaining table. Others learn honesty the hard way (in public), when they get into a publicized position. These are, typically, persons who were *told* what was right and they always were able to *say* what was right, but they had insufficient practice to acquire settled habits and attitudes.

We might as well admit that we came very reluctantly to the Gandhian conclusion that our high schools and colleges are deficient in moral education. There is already a considerable body of literature that argues the need for moral education at all levels.[20] In recent years, since the legal difficulties of religious instruction in public institutions have been reduced, there is widespread discussion of programs for the teaching of morals *and* religion.[21]

The reason that we came to our conclusion reluctantly is that the usual proposal for improving moral instruction is a plan for adding a course—or, God forbid,—a whole new curriculum.[22] That will mean more stuffing of the class schedules with hours and days during which the students talk and listen to talk—mostly, listen to talk.

Our conclusion is, we believe, Gandhian in that it calls for the release of some learning time from talkfests, time for doing something. This will be hard on the teachers, not only because the students may get into trouble, but also because teachers have been trained to lecture, and there is probably a self-selection in recruiting educators; young people who like to talk decide to be teachers.

It may not be too cruel to suggest that teachers bear some resemblance to the actress who had spent several hours telling about her performances in various plays, with appropriate excerpts from the most dramatic lines. At last, she said, "Well, I must not talk about myself so much. What do *you* think of my acting?"

A majority, perhaps, of our high school students have a chance to "belong" to a friendship and action group. In the less affluent neighborhoods, however, the students' gang membership may involve him in activities that will establish habits diametrically opposed to what his school teachers are preaching.

The university years are for large number of students, as Baker Brownell pointed out, years of rootlessness. The class sectioning and housing procedures in many undergraduate colleges could not be more efficiently designed for the prevention of meaningful group activities. The uniform so-many-class-hours-per-week routine further limits the possibilities, and so does the non-partisan pose of the average academic institution.

It is, of course, impossible to stop all action during the years of schooling. It is not surprising that some students fall into activities that establish habits unrelated to their academic studies: drinking, fighting and whoring. Nor is it strange that other students organize for what their elders regard as radical hell-raising.

To be sure, conscientious and resourceful individuals and committees have grappled with the problem. Some progress has been made. The progress to date, it must be admitted, has been in establishing school-related activities that are suitable for young people *who most readily and quickly fit into the more bookish occupations of a specialized, industrial society.* Work-study programs, internships, field work, and assistantships have produced desired results at the senior college, graduate and professional-school levels. Even in these programs there have been difficulties and, often, high costs in supervision, partly because so few adults are in the habit of trying to involve beginners in their regular adult work. Supervisors of interns, teaching assistants, and work-study candidates, for example, have to do a lot of persuading to get some adults to take on apprentices; and, they have to do policing, to keep the apprentices from being exploited as menial laborers, denied any assignments that make for personal development. And, of course, there is a perpetual struggle to fit the extra-curricular activity into the university calendar and daily schedule.

There are Vista and Peace Corps-type jobs that could be taken on by teen-agers; town clean-up campaigns, tutoring, supervising the play of younger children, gathering information needed by public agencies, etc. There are other civic tasks that often don't get done: verifying voter lists, raising money for neighborhood improvements, and the like. There are numerous activities that simply are not in regular budgets, such as, headstart programs in many districts, nursery schools, the kind of work that volunteers can perform in hospitals and libraries, ordinary house work for families crippled by chronic illness, stray dog and cat catching for animal shelters, leg work in connection with celebrations, etc. There are also unbudgeted and unperformed tasks in profitmaking organizations.

If we ask why more young people are not involved in these activities, the answers are along the following lines:

1. The most personable and attractive teachers are busy with regular class work. If they undertake the organization of special projects, they must do so in their spare time.
2. Many adults do not wish to "turn a bunch of youngsters loose." There is an intolerance of any originality or initiative that may be displayed by the young.
3. The time spent sitting in class is sacrosanct. The extras must be sandwiched between classes, and the sandwiches are different for every pair of students.
4. The importance of learning by doing is simply not appreciated. Particularly among teachers, there must be a pay-off in technical skill. The development of sentiments and habits is taken for granted.
5. Except for athletics, the budgets for student activities are

microscopic. There is nearly always a shortage of funds for projects requiring travel.

The first main conclusion regarding moral education, accordingly, is that, regardless of our opinion of the preaching and scripture-reading that is done in the classroom, our educational institutions are denying many students an opportunity to engage in the kind of activities that build a desirable character. The most obvious denials are in the case of the drop-outs; the less obvious denials affect the mine-run of students who do not "wake up" during their school years. We can take comfort in the knowledge that some of these moral failures will be remedied after the students leave school. But is it really necessary that so many should have habit-forming experiences and commitment-creating challenges only by unplanned accident?

The second main conclusion regarding moral education is that our secondary schools and higher institutions of learning are geared for inaction, or, rather, for spinning their wheels when they have to go off of the well-paved academic routines. The recent confrontations between angry students and angry administrators are clear symptoms of the need to change something. But anyone, *anyone*, who has a suggestion, faces a year-long struggle and possibly a ten-year struggle to get his proposal through the machinery of academe. It makes little difference, in the larger institutions, whether the proponent is a student, a junior instructor or the chief executive officer: most of the remedies, and especially the curriculum remedies, for the riot-generating malaise can be adopted only by the consent of what Calhoun called "concurrent majorities."

As we admitted earlier, there was a time when this elaborate set of controls raised standards by regulating the details of instruction and student life. Now, that a large teaching staff possesses the formal credentials for their jobs, it is doubtful that such complicated checks and balances are needed. And it is certain that the system is self-defeating when it comes to the need for innovation.

Aware of this organizational impasse, some few teachers join with the "New Left" and the "Black militants" in poorly directed demonstrations. More of the teachers and not a few administrators settle down on the sidelines. They may be like the Abbé Siéyès, who was an eloquent orator before the French Revolution. During the Revolution he dropped out of sight. After the Terror a friend recognized him on the street and asked, "What did you do during the Revolution?" The Abbé replied, "I survived."

Our conclusion is that the confrontations of the sixties have exposed some inadequacies in moral education. The common *doctrine* holds 1) that all men have rights and that 2) it is desirable to reduce the amount of violence when men quarrel over their respective rights. Much of the instruction in general education and in the professional schools concerns the social organization and technical skills by which destructive warfare is prevented. But this teaching appears not to have been very helpful in the recent difficulties.

The eruption of violence in our high schools and colleges obviously shows that there are *students* whose attitudes have not been much affected by the doctrines of the school men. But some of the *educators* themselves seem not to have been taking their own teachings very seriously. They have let their own institutions become unresponsive to changing interests and so inflexible in their cumbersome procedures that policy changes require more personal sacrifices than the average teacher and the average administrator are prepared to make.

The merely verbal nature of much moral education is exposed by a comparison of the prevalent polite learning with the earnestness and dedication of Mahatma Gandhi. If America is in trouble and if the American educational institutions are in trouble, there is good reason to look to Gandhi's way of grappling with the problems of social conflict. The good reason is not that Gandhi necessarily envisioned an ideal school system for America. His craft-oriented education and his proposal for throwing the engineering schools out of the university may be bad ideas for the United States. But Gandhi's understanding of the connection between theory and practice suggests that some of us who have been very clever in lecturing and writing may have missed the point of Aristotle's distinction between practical wisdom and mere cleverness.

The recent confrontations in American schools lay bare a variety of grievances and grudges among the privileged members of our affluent society. Some of the conflicts, of course, concern the extent to which the privileged community should actively champion the cause of underprivileged people.

Those who resort to disobedience can be measured against Gandhi's discipline by asking if they satisfy his rules:

1. Is the issue a moral one? Is it more than a personal desire? Has the criticism offered by opponents been carefully considered?
2. Has an attempt been made to secure agreement by lawful means?
3. Is the opponent being informed of the plan to use disobedience?
4. Is hatred avoided by sincerely trying to bring the opponent to the right? Is this intent to persuade the opponent implemented by not taking advantage of his temporary misfortunes and embarrassments?
5. Is the penalty of disobedience willingly suffered?
6. Is the disobedience sustained by a discipline of carnal desires?

Those who are the target of disobedience can be measured against Gandhi's standards by asking whether they have deviated from his rules, too:

7. Is violence avoided?
8. What efforts have been made to convince the disobedient that their demand is not a moral one? Have the opponents' criticisms been carefully considered?
9. Has the opponent of the disobedient thought of some form of disobedience which he can use to show his sincerity and for which he willingly accepts the penalty?
10. In resisting the demand, is secrecy of tactics avoided?
11. Is hatred avoided? Is a resumption of amicable relations seriously desired?
12. Are the inconveniences and dangers willingly accepted in the line of duty?

The strictness of Gandhi's discipline was emphasized in countless editorials and speeches. Occasionally, the discipline was spelled out in a list of rules, as in the article published in the paper, *Young India*, on the twenty-seventh of February 1930.[23]

Among Americans, who more or less accept Gandhi's principle of nonviolence, there are obviously disagreements concerning the circumstances that justify the use of active disobedience. Some go all the way with Gandhi's assertion of the right to disobey rules on the sole ground that the individual believes the issue to be an important wrong. Others would limit the resort to disobedience to those who have been denied participation or representation in the rule-making process and to those who have been denied the usual legal remedies.[24]

Disagreements of this sort, however, are overshadowed by the obvious unpopularity of the principle of absolute nonviolence. The confrontations on the American campus reveal differences in the reluctance to use coercion, but less willingness than is now found in union-management industrial relations to negotiate and to sweat it out until there is some meeting of minds and wills. Anyone who is committed to nonviolence will search for tactics that neither *a*) coerce the opposition nor *b*) capitulate to demands that are believed to be wrong. In the conflicts on the campus this means refraining from arson, mass picketing and kidnapping (tactics that have been employed by students) and the avoidance of police charges, expulsion without a hearing, and lockouts (tactics that have been employed by school authorities). To find a Gandhian "experiment" that avoids both violence and a peace-at-any-price surrender requires both stubbornness and imagination, particularly when the opposition is using coercive tactics.

One further comment may emphasize the toughness or hardheadedness of Gandhian behavior in a campus confrontation. Gandhi never suggested that rule breakers should escape punishment. The *Satyagrahi* expects to be punished when he breaks rules nonviolently. The violent rule breaker deserves a penalty, though a Gandhian would certainly look for a penalty that does not depend upon violence.

9

Can There Be a Real Community?

IF THE Gandhi Centennial had been celebrated ten or twenty years ago, American teachers and students would have measured their practices by his standards and might have become conscious of somewhat different deficiencies than those which we have delineated. Even today, we know that the issues upon which we have meditated would not be regarded as the most important issues by some of our colleagues. We have said almost nothing, for example, about international diplomacy and international economic developments. In the opinion of some of our colleagues, Gandhi's challenge to instruction and research in the international field is at least as disturbing as his questioning of the practices on which we have concentrated.[1] The fact that Gandhi, through his recorded words, needles us in so many places is an indication of the depth and breadth of his vision of life in the twentieth century.

In bringing the report of our inquiry to a close, we realize that we have made a very incomplete study of Gandhi's career and a very incomplete review of the meaning of that career for ourselves. We shall consider the effort well spent, if our readers see a little more clearly how Gandhi still helps men to "experiment with truth." We believe that he sensed the unpreparedness of statesmen and professors as well as of ordinary mortals, an unpreparedness for the turbulence of the world in his day and the visible future. The radical sincerity of his attempt to meet the threat of violence under new conditions is still disturbing. It is hard to take. But it should jolt us out of our mental and emotional ruts, as we try to decide what part we should play in the shaping of the future.

We have dwelt at length upon the relation of the schools to the industrialization of society and some of the nasty racial conflicts that are involved in that complicated matter. We do not endorse all of Gandhi's opinions about industrialization. Our society is, perhaps seventy-five or eighty percent "modernized." Gandhi could hardly imagine all that would be at stake in such a society. He spent most of his life addressing people who were not members of such a social order. Yet, his strong assertions have some relevance to our predicament. He denounced an industrial system that left the Indian peasants out of the technology and left them out, so far as most of the benefits were concerned. We in America in 1969 are aware that some people have been "left out" of our system. Gandhi-inspired educators and students can, we believe, ask some of the right questions and, perhaps, correct some of the wrong answers in the controversies that relate to this massive maladjustment.

As we leave the reader to his own further reflections we should like to call attention to one additional facet of Gandhian "truth." It presents us with what appears to be a logical contradiction and, if the contradiction cannot be explained away, it might undercut everything that Gandhi said about nonviolence. We refer to his faith in the oneness of all life and his simultaneous lack of faith in big organizations.

This seems to be the same paradox that shows up in the thinking of our more romantic western prophets. "The universal brotherhood of man" arouses great expectations among the romantics, but all of the more inclusive institutions now in existence are dismissed with a phrase that has become an epithet of contempt. They are "the Establishment." Governments, federations, corporations, markets, and alliances are said to be unsound *in principle*. They cannot satisfy the moral aspirations of men "at the grass roots." They do perform some welfare functions, but the modern state is not really becoming a "welfare state." It is a power-and-pressure-group state. Welfare gets attention only when organized pressures demand it.[2]

Western critics and prophets, who denounce existing institutions, often seem to expect some entirely different kind of social relationships to replace the hard-line organizational life of today. Instead of placing their bets on the United Nations, various inter-governmental arrangements and the corporations that have "gone international," they talk about a "people-to-people" program. To replace the bureaucracy-ridden domestic programs of state, school and church, they talk about the "real communities" of the future. They look forward to a recovery of the genuine charity that characterized many townships, churches, hospitals, and labor unions before they became big and wealthy.

In Gandhi's case, the social unit that was romantically glorified was the traditional Indian village. It was to the village that Gandhi looked for the humanizing morality that would make men fit to live with one another. The village, rather than soulless corporations and headless governments, would nurture respect for *Ahimsa*.

We have already conceded that Gandhi is correct in identifying small-group life as the matrix of morality, the indispensable agency in moral education. We are in at least partial agreement also with his characterization of big industrialized and urbanized institutions. They cannot fully satisfy our moral aspirations. What, then, becomes of this dream of an all-inclusive brotherhood, if the most inclusive human organizations yet devised are so unideal? Is the "oneness of all life" some sort of irrationalism, a myth of the twentieth century?

No, there is no paradox in Gandhi's hopes, although there may be a contradiction in the thinking of people who sound like Gandhi. Gandhi did not assume that all of the villages in the world were ever going to find themselves in complete agreement. If for no other reason, conflict could be expected to persist because of human fallibility. Gandhi never attributed perfect knowledge to himself and he certainly did not attribute it to any other mere mortal. That was the point of his oft-reiterated assertion about the need for making "experiments."

Gandhi never asserted that all humanity could live together without conflict. All that he contended was that conflict need not be violent. Indeed, he was convinced that under the then-developing conditions, humanity would destroy itself unless it learned how to keep conflict nonviolent.

We, who find ourselves in a country that is already urbanized and industrialized, may be justified in doubting what Gandhi said about the self-sufficiency of villages. But we should not, on that account, discount his insistence on small-group life as the source of moral aspirations that correct the dehumanizing tendencies in large-scale institutions.

In the place of peasant villages we should, perhaps, put our faith in other agencies that have the virtues of building morale and accustoming human beings to one another. We may not be ingenious enough to find suitable work groups for all of our drop-outs and ghetto-dwellers; and perhaps, that kind of occupational fraternity is not desirable for everyone. But we can hardly expect a person to respect humanity at large, if he respects no one in his vicinity, including himself.

So far as educational institutions are to be judged by Gandhi's standards, and they are the object of our immediate concern, we can see that insufficient attention has been given to "the villages," the smallest units in any public school system and any university. If, now, we commit more of our capital and more of ourselves to this personal side of schooling, we shall continue to need Gandhi's reminders. The moral motivations, that are established in small-group living, ought not encyst themselves in the asylum of our little *Ashram*. They must address themselves to public affairs, to the great issues of justice and power that take us all beyond the congenial circle of like-minded friends and relatives. And that is why the commitment to nonviolence needs to be open, experimental, and truth-seeking.

Epilogue

by N. A. NIKAM

THIS PHILOSOPHICAL study of Gandhi is outstandingly significant in its interpretation of Gandhi's "experiment" with truth. Its exposition is lucid and coherent, compact and terse. And the book reveals an understanding insight in discussing the relevance of Gandhi and the novelty of his method to the conflicts, tensions and novel situations of the contemporary world. In this epilogue I want to bring into focus some of the many significant points that the authors make in their discussion of the Gandhian philosophy or way of life.

Professors Wayne Leys and P. S. S. Rama Rao make the significant statement that the Gandhian philosophy is essentially a philosophy of action. Gandhi is a mystic of action. The *Gita* says, we cannot withdraw from action. And when we act, we act for the future. The future is an exploration of ourselves; as the authors say, it is an exploration of our value systems. The authors are right in saying that in our study of the future or in acting for the future, Gandhi will help. For, the future that Gandhi contemplated is very different from the future contemplated by most of us; it is the future as contemplated by Gandhi that will bring security, peace and freedom.

The authors say that Gandhi was essentially a religious man; it is as a religious man that he approached problems of human relations in his philosophy of action. But, what is religion to Gandhi? Religion is to Gandhi a quest of truth. There are two questions to be distinguished in Gandhi's "experiment" with Truth: *a*) What is Truth?; and *b*) How to attain Truth? Gandhi answered the first by answering the second. We attain truth through nonviolence. It is in his quest for Truth that Gandhi says he discovered nonviolence. Nonviolence is a means or the only means to Truth. And the Truth to which nonviolence is a means is nonviolence: this is the paradox involved in Gandhi's conception of means and ends, central to his philosophy of action.

The authors are right in saying that Gandhi transformed non-violence from the "ethic of perfection" or salvation to the "ethic of action," from the conception of a means to individual salvation to a means of collective action, from undergoing self-suffering as a part of the discipline of the ethic of perfection to a conscious suffering for the sake of others as part of the ethic of action. Gandhi called this *Satyagraha*. *Satyagraha* is truth in action. *Satyagraha* is resistance, resistance to evil. *Satyagraha* is action, not non-action. As Gandhi said, *Satyagraha* is a "non-violence of the *brave*," not a "non-violence of the weak." Professors Wayne Leys and P. S. S. Rama Rao sum up the essence of *Satyagraha* in these words: "*Satyagraha* is an achievement; it is not a miraculous gift. It is achieved by deeply religious men who do not run away from society. The *Satyagrahi* is not dependent upon an existing society for his ideals. Yet his immediate objectives are determined by an imaginative study of the society in which he happens to dwell." While, on the one hand, *Satyagraha* is following one's own conscience; on the other, it is a consciousness of the common good and its promotion in a peaceful and constructive way.

The authors discover Gandhi's strength in his character. They say that while Gandhi's character made him a great man, his identification with the masses made him a great leader, but they point out that Gandhi was not a "follower" of his followers. Gandhi was a man who could say no to the masses. In Gandhi, duties come first, and rights afterwards. The openness of Truth that Gandhi discovered in his experiments with Truth left him with no strategy. As Gandhi's policies were derived from his religion, the authors make the significant statement that Gandhi manifested the rare possibility of a man becoming a statesman by becoming a saint.

Is a nonviolent social order possible? Is it all "non-cooperation?" Even if a nonviolent social order is possible, there would still be room for vigilance. A nonviolent social order depends upon individual vigilance. It involves peaceful, constructive, creative cooperation. Therefore, Gandhi's nonviolent way of life has a constructive side; this is his conception of work, and his conception of education. Gandhi's conception of work involves the philosophy of "Bread-Labor," no able-bodied man has a *right* to eat if he does not do some work, and all work, according to Gandhi, is noble, and all work ought to transcend into a *yajna*, "sacrifice;" all work is to become dedicated work. Education is to Gandhi, character building, and all education is moral education, and Gandhi's conception of education is the same as his conception of means and ends. The pursuit of human ends involves a person in social conflicts, and in these conflicts everyone has a choice of means, and nonviolent means are instrumental in avoiding war, and nonviolent means are also a way to a person's self-improvement.

Nehru said that there was something "unpredictable" in Gandhi. We may say that part of this unpredictability came from Gandhi's mystical conception of Truth: Gandhi's conception of absolute truth made nothing absolute. Gandhi's non-cooperation could become willing cooperation. Therefore, I agree with the statement that there is nothing inherently and intrinsically right in a boycott; that a hunger strike or an authorised march will be everywhere and under all conditions a tactic worthy of Gandhi. Professors Wayne Leys and P. S. S. Ramo Rao say that while we cannot "imitate" Gandhi, we cannot consider Gandhi "irrelevant." Gandhi is not "irrelevant" because we need something of the character that Gandhi had: the extraordinary ability to look within himself and overcome the stubborn opposition within himself if that stood in the way of reconciliation. And the authors say that Gandhi would have added the proposition "criticise thyself as thy neighbor" to the proposition "love thy neighbor as thyself."

Since there is always troubled conscience, and as troubled conscience ought to issue in action, a program of nonviolent action involves selection of proper targets for a Gandhian attack so that it is capable of a visible response. Otherwise, as

Gandhi said, *Satyagraha* degenerates into what he called, *duragraha*, evil action. Therefore, the selection of proper targets is a creative step that involves as the authors say mystical insights of dedicated individuals like Gandhi.

This study on Gandhi points out that civil disobedience as an alternative to violence has European and American origins independent of Gandhi. Americans are acquainted with non-violent civil disobedience. While there is some acquaintance in America with civil disobedience as a nonviolent technique, the stubborn difficulty, as the authors say, that Dr. Martin Luther King, experienced in his advocacy of civil disobedience "was infusing disobedience with the love of the enemy, a Christian and Gandhian freedom from hatred." This means that nonviolent civil disobedience is very much more than a technique; nonviolence is a way of life; it is a way of living; that it is not merely a technique but a way of living was what was involved in Gandhi's experiment with Truth that he conducted in the way life was ordered in his hermitage or *ashram*. The *ashram* was an "experiment in living." Nonviolence is not merely a technique but is involved in a way of life; the way of life that it involves is involved in the recovery of a faith and in living a faith that is already there. And so, the Gandhi Centennial catches American teachers and students, as the authors say, at a moment when they may be in a mood to give more than a polite gesture in the direction of Gandhian love and self-sacrifice. This is a discovery which is, indeed, good news. Therefore, this enquiry at Southern Illinois University has been rewarding and worth while.

Carbondale, Illinois   N. A. Nikam
February, 1969

.

Notes

CHAPTER 1

1. Bertrand de Jouvenel, *The Art of Conjecture*, (New York, 1967). See, among others, Daniel Bell et al., "Toward the Year 2000," *Daedalus XCVI*, 3 (Summer, 1967), also, H. Kahn and A. J. Wiener, *The Year 2000* (New York, 1967).
2. We are indebted to Dr. Charles Tenney, Vice President for Planning and Review at Southern Illinois University, for calling our attention to a number of studies of the future.

CHAPTER 2

1. M. K. Gandhi, *All Men Are Brothers* (New York, 1958), p. 56.
2. *Ibid.*, p. 71.
3. M. K. Gandhi, *Non-Violent Resistance* (New York, 1967), pp. 38–39.
4. *Ibid.*, p. 1.
5. M. K. Gandhi, *All Men Are Brothers*, p. 75.
6. M. K. Gandhi, *Non-Violent Resistance*, p. 42.
7. S. Radhakrishnan, *Indian Philosophy* (London, 1929), I, 327.
8. M. K. Gandhi, *All Men Are Brothers*, p. 107.
9. *Ibid.*, pp. 100–101.
10. *Ibid.*, p. 101.
11. M. K. Gandhi, *All Men Are Brothers*, p. 105.
12. Martin Luther King, Jr., *Stride Toward Freedom* (New York, 1958), p. 78.
13. M. K. Gandhi, *All Men Are Brothers*, p. 88.
14. *Ibid.*, p. 87.
15. *Ibid.*, p. 86.
16. *Ibid.*, p. 93.
17. *Ibid.*, p. 89.
18. *Ibid.*, p. 93.
19. *Ibid.*, p. 102.
20. *Ibid.*, pp. 106–07.
21. *Ibid.*, p. 77.
22. M. K. Gandhi, *Non-Violent Resistance*, p. 36.
23. M. K. Gandhi, *To The Students* (Ahmedabad, 1949), p. 147.
24. *Ibid.*, p. 165.
25. *Ibid.*, pp. 165–66.
26. *Ibid.*, p. 167.
27. *Ibid.*, p. 270. The question of "academic freedom" in so far as teachers are concerned is rather a new phenomenon and did not bother Gandhi much. He had some occasional comments to make, never-

theless. Somewhere he says: "What the schoolmaster resents, and rightly, is espionage and suppression of free thought." (*Ibid.*, p. 260). Professor Willis Moore sees that "in the institution of intellectual freedom we have one of the great inventions of mankind, an invention by means of which men are able not only to harmonize divergent views through peaceful discussion but, more importantly, to profit by these very divergencies in a way not open to the adherents of any totalitarian methodology." "Causal Factors in the Current Attack on Education", *Bulletin of the American Association of University Professors*, XLI (Winter 1955), 628.

28. A substantial portion of the material in this part of Chapter II was taken from our paper, "Gandhi's Synthesis of Indian Spirituality and Western Politics," to be shortly published by Atherton Press in *Nomos*, Volume XI, edited by Roland Pennock and John Chapman.
29. M. K. Gandhi, *Non-Violent Resistance*, p. 35.
30. *Ibid.*, p. 1.
31. *Ibid.*
32. M. K. Gandhi, *All Men Are Brothers*, p. 99.
33. M. K. Gandhi, *Non-Violent Resistance*, p. 4.
34. *Ibid.*, p. 238.
35. *Ibid.*, p. 294.
36. *Ibid.*, p. 174.
37. *Ibid.*
38. M. K. Gandhi, *All Men Are Brothers*, p. 88.
39. M. K. Gandhi, *Non-Violent Resistance*, pp. 193–94.
40. M. K. Gandhi, *Autobiography* or *The Story of My Experiment with Truth* (Washington D.C., 1948) p. 184.
41. M. K. Gandhi, *Non-Violent Resistance*, p. 29.
42. *Ibid.*, p. 174.
Gandhi was certainly aware of the undesirability of anarchy and civil war. After helping the Kheda agriculturalists to overcome their fears he recognized the urgent necessity of persuading them to avoid incivility. On many later occasions he denounced the *Goondas* (ruffians) who joined in his demonstrations. He advised against mass picketing ("a living wall of pickets") as naked violence. In 1942, he opposed plans for a scorched earth policy in the event of a Japanese invasion. ("There is no bravery in my poisoning my well or filling it in so that my brother who is at war with me may not use the water.") This restraint was in line with his 1920 opposition to "social boycott." At that time he had said, "It would be totally opposed to the doctrine of non-violence to stop the supply of water and food." When *Goondaism* made its appearance during his Civil Disobedience campaigns, Gandhi not only denounced the coercive tactics: on several occasions he used *Satyagraha* against people who thought they were his allies. Gandhi's emphasis upon the word "civil" in "Civil Disobedience" was consistently strong.
At the same time, Gandhi was equally insistent on the universal right of conscientious disobedience. He rejected the principle of "majority rule" on the grounds that the inner voice of conscience should be followed even when it opposed laws that had been democratically enacted by a governmental majority. Gandhi did not see this right of conscience as an invitation to civil war, or as in any way giving moral sanction to the State's employment of coercive police powers.

43. M. K. Gandhi, *Non-Violent Resistance*, p. 18.
44. *Ibid.*
45. *Ibid.*, p. 313.
46. M. K. Gandhi, *All Men Are Brothers*, pp. 89–90.
47. See, for example, Sasadhar Sinha, *Indian Independence in Perspective* (New York, 1960).
48. Quoted in Hiren Mukherjee, *Gandhiji: A Study* (Calcutta, 1958), p. 134.
49. Arne Naess, *Gandhi and the Nuclear Age* (Totowa, N.J., 1965), p. 13. Arne Naess gives a number of such examples from Gandhi's life. See, especially, Part I.

CHAPTER 3

1. M. K. Gandhi, *All Men Are Brothers* (New York, 1958), p. 46.
2. M. K. Gandhi, *Autobiography or The Story of My Experiments with Truth* (Washington, D.C., 1948), p. 33.
3. M. K. Gandhi, *Autobiography*, p. 81.
4. J. Nehru, *Toward Freedom: The Autobiography of Jawaharlal Nehru* (Boston, 1961), p. 31.
5. M. K. Gandhi, *Autobiography*, p. 120.
6. *Ibid.*, p. 129.
7. Quoted in E. Stanley Jones, *Mahatma Gandhi: An Interpretation* (New York and Nashville, 1948), p. 83.
8. M. K. Gandhi, *Autobiography*, pp. 26–27.
9. J. Nehru, *Mahatma Gandhi* (New York, 1966), p. 69.
10. M. K. Gandhi, *All Men Are Brothers*, p. 144.
11. E. S. Jones, *Mahatma Gandhi: An Interpretation*, p. 17.
12. M. K. Gandhi, *All Men Are Brothers*, p. 58.
13. *Ibid.*, p. 76.
14. J. Nehru, *Mahatma Gandhi*, p. 76.
15. *Ibid.*, p. 46.
16. M. K. Gandhi, *All Men Are Brothers*, p. 144.
17. Nehru, J., *Mahatma Gandhi*, p. 103.
18. *Ibid.*, p. 72.
19. *Ibid.*, p. 104.
20. J. Nehru, *Mahatma Gandhi*, p. 122.
21. E. Stanley Jones, *Mahatma Gandhi: An Interpretation* p. 33.
22. M. K. Gandhi, *Autobiography*, p. 5.
23. M. K. Gandhi, *Non-Violent Resistance* (New York, 1961), pp. 29–30.
24. *Ibid.*, p. 234.
25. M. K. Gandhi, *All Men Are Brothers*, p. 4.
26. Quoted in G. N. Dhawan, *The Political Philosophy of Mahatma Gandhi* (Ahmedabad, 1957), p. 209.
27. Quoted in Hiren Mukherjee, *Gandhiji: A Study* (Calcutta, 1958), p. 139.
28. M. K. Gandhi, *All Men Are Brothers*, p. 81.
29. J. Nehru, *Mahatma Gandhi*, p. 44.
30. *Ibid.*, p. 41.
31. M. K. Gandhi, *All Men Are Brothers*, p. 53.
32. Arnold Toynbee, *One World and India* (New Delhi, 1960), pp. 50ff.

33. R. C. Majumdar, *History of the Freedom Movement in India* (Calcutta: Firma K. L. Mukhopadhyay, 1963), III, p. xxiii.
34. *Ibid.*, p. xxiv.
35. *Ibid.*

C H A P T E R   4

1. M. K. Gandhi, *Towards New Education* (Ahmedabad, 1956), p. 9.
2. M. K. Gandhi, *Basic Education* (Ahmedabad, 1956), p. 37.
3. M. K. Gandhi, *Towards New Education*, p. 44.
4. M. K. Gandhi, *All Men Are Brothers* (New York, 1958), p. 157.
5. M. K. Gandhi, *Basic Education*, pp. 29–30.
6. D. G. Tendulkar, *Mahatma* (New Delhi, 1961), II, 99.
7. M. K. Gandhi, *Basic Education*, pp. 49–50.
8. M. K. Gandhi, *All Men Are Brothers*, p. 124.
9. M. K. Gandhi, *Basic Education*, p. 47.
10. M. K. Gandhi, *Towards New Education*, p. 42.
11. M. K. Gandhi, *Basic Education*, pp. 50–51.
12. Jawaharlal Nehru, *The Discovery of India* (London, 1956), p. 571.
13. *Ibid.*
14. *Ibid.*, p. 414.
15. *Ibid.*, p. 415.
16. M. K. Gandhi, *All Men Are Brothers*, p. 129.
17. *Ibid.*, p. 140.
18. George E. Axtelle, "John Dewey and the Genius of American Civilization," *John Dewey and the World View*, ed. Douglas E. Lawson and Arthur E. Lean (Carbondale, Ill., 1964), p. 59.
19. M. K. Gandhi, *To The Students* (Ahmedabad, 1949), p. 291.
20. M. K. Gandhi, *Autobiography* or *The Story of My Experiments With Truth* (Washington, D.C., 1948), p. 408.
21. M. K. Gandhi, *To The Students*, p. 107.
22. *Ibid.*, p. 122.
23. M. K. Gandhi, *All Men Are Brothers*, p. 75.
24. *Ibid.*, p. 56.
25. M. K. Gandhi, *Basic Education*, p. 105.
26. *Ibid.*, p. 106.
27. M. K. Gandhi, *Towards New Education*, p. 79.
28. *Ibid.*, p. 79.
29. *Ibid.*, p. 81.
30. *Ibid.*
31. M. K. Gandhi, *All Men Are Brothers*, p. 177.

C H A P T E R   5

1. Remarks of Dr. George Brock Chisholm, for many years Director General of the World Health Organization, *Social Service Review*, XXXVI (June 1962), 195, 196.
2. Thurman W. Arnold, *The Folklore of Capitalism* (New Haven, Conn., 1937), p. 14.
3. Arne Naess, *Gandhi and the Nuclear Age* (Totowa, N.J., 1965). See also Harry Prosch, "Toward an Ethics of Civil Disobedience," *Ethics*, LXXVII (April 1967), 176–92. Prosch thinks that approval of the right

of civil disobedience may rest more on a faith in democracy than on a philosophical commitment, at least in the case of Westerners.

Hugo Bedau has argued that "it is difficult to see how one could produce principles laying down the sufficient and necessary conditions for the practice of civil disobedience in all situations." "On Civil Disobedience," *Journal of Philosophy*, LVIII, 21 (1961).

CHAPTER 6

1. John Kenneth Galbraith, *The New Industrial State* (Boston, 1967).
2. See James Ridgeway, "Universities as Big Business," *Harper's* magazine, September 1968. For readers who are getting bored with the somber tone of all this, we recommend Arthur E. Lean's *And Merely Teach* (Carbondale, Ill., 1968).
3. George S. Counts, *Educacão para uma sociedade de homens livres an era tecnologica* (Rio de Janeiro, 1958), pp. 78–79.
4. See *Perspectives in Mental Retardation*, ed. T. E. Jordan (Carbondale, Ill., 1966). See also L. Wilbur, *Vocations for the Visually Handicapped* (New York, 1937), and I. and A. Ewing, *Opportunity and the Deaf Child* (London, 1947, 1950).
5. "Changing Directions in American Education," *Saturday Review*, January 14, 1967. There are, of course, many pressures in the direction of lower standards in the United States. In some of the "new nations," educational qualifications for office have been virtually abolished. This also happened in the United States and elsewhere during the nineteenth century, when political control was wrested from the old land-holding aristocracy. College entrance requirements were also reduced, as in the land-grant colleges. This sort of "democratization" was feared by men like Alexis de Tocqueville and was ridiculed by representatives of the "old learning," like Barrett Wendell, who proposed that the Bachelor of Arts degree be conferred upon every child at birth. The industry-minded men, who now resist an equalization of opportunity by lowering standards, are conscious not only of the technical problems of management but also of the skill required in nonmanagerial jobs.
6. The U. S. government began some years ago, a series of job training programs, starting in the state of West Virginia, with rather unimpressive results. In 1967 the big automotive companies in Detroit began intensive recruiting and training among Negroes who did not have the qualifications usually required, and, a year later, were issuing mildly optimistic reports.
7. See Chapter V, "The Educated Society," in Peter F. Drucker's *Landmarks of Tomorrow* (New York, 1958). When President Delyte W. Morris established an Area Services Division at Southern Illinois University, he quoted Arthur Morgan's 1953 prophecy: "Here in Southern Illinois you are at the beginning of an industrial era. Some parts of the country have fifty years' head start of you." (See G. K. Plochmann, *The Ordeal of Southern Illinois University* (Carbondale, Ill., 1959), I, 143.
8. See Baker Brownell, *The Human Community* (New York, 1950); *The College and the Community* (New York, 1952); *The Other Illinois* (New York, 1958).

9. Edward Banfield, *The Moral Basis of a Backward Society*, (Glencoe, 1958); *Government Project*, (Glencoe, 1951). Richard Waverly Poston, in his book, *Democracy Speaks with Many Tongues*, (New York, 1962), expressed dismay over the "failure" of American foreign aid because it had financed physical plants and "built everything but communities and democratic societies," with the result that "the forces of social unrest and regimentation have moved forward." (p. 47) Our view of this difficult subject was influenced by discussions in an interdisciplinary seminar, as reported in "Developing International Resources to Assist with Educational Planning," by Robert Jacobs, F. G. Macomber, and G. C. Wiegand, (Southern Illinois University, Mimeo, 1963).

10 There is an immense literature expressing and analyzing these morale difficulties. Some of it comes from outside the United States, as, for example, Frantz Fanon's *Black Skin, White Masks* (1952). Here are a few of the writings, though it is risky to say that they are representative:

Lorraine Hansberry, *The Movement* (New York, 1964).
Louis Lomax, *The Negro Revolt* (New York, 1962).
James Baldwin, *The Fire Next Time* (New York, 1963).
Claude Brown, *Manchild in the Promised Land* (New York, 1965).
Ralph Creger, *A Look Down the Lonesome Road* (New York, 1964).
Dick Gregory, *The Shadow that Scares Me* (New York, 1968).
Neil Hickey and Ed Edwin, *Adam Clayton Powell and the Politics of Race* (New York, 1965).
LeRoi Jones, *Home: Social Essays* (New York, 1966).
Malcolm Little, *The Autobiography of Malcolm X* (New York, 1965).
Claude Nolen, *The Negro's Image in the South* (Lexington, Ky., 1967).
D. P. Ausubel, "Ego Development Among Segregated Negro Children," *Mental Hygiene*, XLII (1958), 362–69.
R. J. Havighurst, "Who Are the Socially Disadvantaged?", *The Journal of Negro Education*, XXXIII (1964), 210–17.
S. J. Rackstraw and W. P. Robinson, "Social and Psychological Factors Related to the Variability of Answering Behavior in Five-Year-Old Children," *Language and Speech*, X (April-June 1967), 88–106.
D. P. Ausubel, "The Effects of Cultural Deprivation on Learning Patterns," *Education and Social Crisis*, ed. E. T. Keach et al. (New York, 1967), pp. 156–61.
W. C. Kvaraceus et al., *The Relationship of Education to Self-Concept in Negro Children and Youth* (New York, 1965).
J. Siller, "Socio-Economic Status and Conceptual Thinking," *Journal of Abnormal and Social Psychology*, LV (1967), 365–71.
Robert G. Brown, "Comparisons of Vocational Aspirations of Paired Sixth Grade White and Negro Children Who Attended Segregated Schools," *Journal of Educational Research*, LVIII (1965), 402–04.
S. Lichter, et. al., *The Drop-Outs* (New York, 1962).

These items have been selected from a much longer bibliography prepared by Colin De'ath, Michael Gibbons, and Earnest O'Neil for the International and Development Education Program of the University of Pittsburgh. We are grateful for the leads thus provided into many interesting lines of study.

The point, we reiterate, is that the facts revealed in this literature are not assimilated into instructional programs when the history, English, and sociology departments study pertinent books in courses with the usual orientation. As Professor Stuart Taylor has said, "Instruction usually is pitched to the understanding and values of the upper middle-class student by teachers who continue to attend universities that perpetuate virtually the same system, biases, courses, and methods of the 1930's." (Address reported in *The Daily Egyptian*, December 4, 1968).

11. Thedford Slaughter, "Up from Hate," *Saturday Review*, December 16, 1967, p. 59.
12. B. Brownell, *The Human Community* (New York, 1950).
13. See *Learning and World Peace*, Eighth Symposium, The Conference on Science, Philosophy, and Religion, (New York, 1948) p. 356.
14. Buckminster Fuller's autobiographical article, "Man with a Chronofile," is a persuasive statement of his point of view. See *Saturday Review*, April 1, 1967, p. 15.
15. Professor S. Kumar Jain pointed out the error in the frequent identification of Gandhi with a completely anti-industrialization point of view.
16. We are confronted here with the difference between the complexity of the administrative point of view and the need for apparent simplicity in the point of view of a partisan or advocate, as well as the simplicity of the specialized expert's point of view. Professor Frank Thomas has made us aware of these different points of view in an article, "Economically Distressed Areas and the Role of the Academic Geographer," *The Professional Geographer*, XIV (March, 1962), 12–15. He notes that there may be distressed areas which, objectively viewed, do not warrant the investment of developmental funds and should be permitted to waste away, a judgment that is opposed by other cultural values and by social pressures.

CHAPTER 7

1. See *The Journal of Conflict Resolution* for many interesting studies.
2. In a memorandum to our committee, Professor Robert H. Dreher (Southern Illinois University Center for the Study of Crime and Correction) traced the criticism of excessive force in police work through a series of documents developed at the level of the federal government in 1924 (when the Bureau of Investigation was reorganized as the Federal Bureau of Investigation), in 1931, when Mr. Wickersham reported the findings of the National Commission on Law Observance and Enforcement, to 1967, when the President's Commission on Law Enforcement and Administration of Justice issued its report. The University of California began, in the 1930's (under the leadership of August Vollmer) to set up courses in police administration and similar innovations occurred at Northwestern University and the University of Texas. Now the U.S. Department of Justice finances many training institutes and conferences, which schools like Southern Illinois University organize for police officials. Some progress has been made, but as the police action in some of the 1967 riots indicated, there are still many poorly disciplined police

departments. Surveys, conducted in 1961 and 1964, showed that few cities in the United States have well defined policies regarding the use of firearms, and fewer yet have adequate training programs. See Report on Violence During the 1968 Democratic Convention, The President's Commission on Violence, December 1, 1968. See, also, the symposium: "The Police in a Democratic Society," *Public Administration Review*, XXVIII, 5 (September 1968).

The trend away from corporal punishments in prisons (for violation of prison rules) is documented in Rubin's *The Law of Criminal Corrections* (St. Paul, Minn., 1963), but twenty-six American states still permit lashing, gagging, and more primitive methods of discipline.

3. Joan Bondurant, *The Conquest of Violence* (Princeton, N.J., 1958), p. 232.
4. John Dewey, *Liberalism and Social Action* (New York, 1935).
5. John Dewey, *Human Nature and Conduct* (New York, 1922), p. 228–29. Henry Holt and Co., 1922.
6. Staughton Lynd, *Nonviolence in America: A Documentary History* (Indianapolis, Ind., 1966).
7. See the case study published under that title by the Committee on Public Administration Cases, Washington, D.C., 1949.
8. See Saul Alinsky, *Reveille for Radicals* (Chicago, 1946). See, also, the debates concerning Alinsky's services in numerous books and journals of opinion.
9. See Stokely Carmichael and Charles V. Hamilton, *Black Power: The Politics of Liberation in America* (New York, 1967).
10. Special issue of the *Annals* of the American Academy of Political and Social Science, edited by Marvin E. Wolfgang, Volume 364 (March 1966).

CHAPTER 8

1. Illustrative of the developing literature on the subject of student unrest are the following:

Christopher Jencks and David Riesman, *The Academic Revolution* (New York, 1968);
Crisis at Columbia: Report of the Cox Commission (New York, 1968).
Bertram Davis, "The Campus Upheaval," *AAUP Bulletin*, September 1968.
The Report of the Committee of Seven on *The Campus Disturbance of October 19, 1967*, Brooklyn College, March 1968.
Richard Flacks, "The Liberated Generation: An Exploration of the Roots of Student Protest," *Journal of Social Issues*, XXIII (1968).
George F. Kennan, *Democracy and the Student Left* (Boston, 1968).

The sorting out of grievances under the three headings, mentioned in the text, is taken from the 17-page report of the Committee on Student Affairs of the Southern Illinois (Carbondale) Chapter of the American Association of University Professors, November 18, 1968 (Charles Stalon, Chairman; Tom Davis, Don Ihde, Eugene Traini, and Stuart Taylor).

2. Clark Kerr, "American Education in the Next Two Decades," *Graduate Comment* (Wayne State University), XI (1968), 23.
3. As quoted in *Newsweek*, September 30, 1968, p. 67. The similarity of Hayden's mood to that of a French student leader, Jacques Sauvageot, is striking: "Students are expected to have a certain critical intelligence, while their studies are such that they are not allowed to exercise it. On the other hand, they realize that in a few years' time they will not be able to find a part to play in society that corresponds to their training." See *The French Student Revolt; The Leaders Speak,* ed. Herve Bourges (New York, 1968).
4. *Los Angeles Free Press,* May 1968.
5. Address delivered at American Philosophical Association meeting in St. Louis, Missouri, May 2, 1968, published in *Ethics* LXXIX (October, 1968), 1–9.
6. The insignificance of student government is probably overdrawn. For a correction of this picture, see Gordon Klopf and Dennis Trueblood, "A Study of the Leadership of the United States National Student Association 1947–1960." *The Journal of College Student Personnel,* IV (December 1962), 73–78.
7. Cornelius L. Golightly, "The Negro and Respect for Law," *Chicago Daily Law Bulletin,* April 26, 1968, p. 8. Professor Golightly's statement of the problem anticipated the diagnosis given by Justice A. Fortas in a syndicated newspaper article later in the same year.
8. This statement is quoted from the Educational Records Bureau *Journal* (Fall, 1966).
9. See, for example, William T. Greenwood, *Management and Organization Behavior Theories* (Cincinnati, Ohio, 1965); J. D. Glover and R. M. Hower, *The Administrator* (Homewood, Ill., 1952); J. R. Lawrence et al., *Organizational Behavior and Administration,* (Homewood, Illinois, 1961).
10. See Addison Hickman, "The Entrepreneurial Function: The South as a Case Study," in *Essays in Southern Economic Development,* ed. W. T. Whitman and M. L. Greenhut (Chapel Hill, N.C., 1964). See also the statement of S. H. Barnes in "Leadership Style and Political Competence," *Political Leadership in Industrialized Societies,* ed. L. J. Edinger (New York, 1967).
11. Appeals to do something to avoid the dreadful spectre of nuclear war are typical of the kind of exhortations mentioned here. There is, of course, a voluminous alarmist literature. See H. G. Hillegas, *The Future as Nightmare* (New York, 1967).
12. The words of William James in his *The Principles of Psychology.* The contrast of moral intellectualism and voluntarism is interestingly developed by Frederick A. Olafson in his *Principles and Persons, An Ethical Interpretation of Existentialism* (Baltimore, Md., 1967).
13. Gandhi, *Indian Home Rule,* reprinted in M. K. Gandhi, *Non-violent Resistance* (New York, 1961). Copyright, Navajivan Trust, 1951.
14. Gandhi and the ancient Greek and Roman Stoics do not hold to the same ethical theories on certain points. See W. Leys, *Ethics for Policy Decisions,* Chapter 6, (Englewood Cliffs, N.J., 1952), Chapter 6.
15. See Gandhi, *Autobiography* or *The Story of My Experiment with Truth,* (Washington, D.C., 1948), 216.
16. See our discussion of the problem of selecting a target in Chapter 2.
17. See F. Lilge, *The Abuse of Learning* (New York, 1948).

18. It was the contention of the late William Henry Harris that Gandhi had found a middle way that lay between Koestler's Commissar and Yogi. The Commissar, preoccupied with the achievement of institutional goals, was ready to employ any means to get his job done. The Yogi, concerned only about his own purity, neglected his duties in the public world. Gandhi combined scrupulous avoidance of evil intentions with a social responsibility. See "The Third Way— Gandhi's Answer," *The Unitarian Register*, March 10, 1960.
19. This is a recent elaboration of the views presented in H. N. Wieman, *Man's Ultimate Commitment* (Carbondale, Ill., 1958).

    Professor John Childs presents an interesting statement of the same problem of commitment in *Education for Morals* (New York, 1950), pp. 194–95. Professor Childs recognizes that society will probably keep on churning up new partisan conflicts, making it difficult for anyone to say truthfully, "There is an ideal plan toward which we are all working;" yet we can, Dr. Childs contends, have a general faith in society.

    Chancellor Robert MacVicar has indicated the emotional difficulty with which educators accept the novel obligations of a changing society by comparing us to the rich young man who asked Christ what he had to do in order to be saved. Christ asked if he had kept the Ten Commandments, and he said, "Yes." But when Christ told him to give his property to the poor he went away sorrowfully.
20. A few samples of this literature follow:

    John E. Smith, *Value Convictions in Higher Education* (Hazen Foundation, 1959).
    E. D. Eddy, *The College Influence on Student Character* (American Council on Education, 1959).
    P. E. Jacob, *Changing Values in College* (New York, 1957).
21. *Religious Studies in Public Universities*, ed. Milton McLean (Carbondale, Ill., 1967).
22. A sample of the ingenuity expended in devising new courses will be found in *The Larger Learning: Teaching Values to College Students* ed. Marjorie Carpenter (Dubuque, Iowa, 1960). We think the subtitle is revealing: "teaching to!" Why not "teaching at?"
23. Reprinted in B. Kumarappa's edition of M. K. Gandhi, *Non-Violent Resistance* (New York, 1961, 1967).
24. See, for example, the papers of John Rawls and others in *Law and Philosophy*, ed. Sidney Hook, (New York, 1964). Some of the American writers who restrict severely the right of disobedience seem to forget the time-honored right of testing the legality of a statute or an executive order. Reminders of this right are presented in W. Leys, "Ethics and the Rule of Law," *Annals* of the American Academy 343 (September, 1962), 32–38; and in Justice Abe Fortas, *Concerning Dissent and Civil Disobedience*, (New York, 1968).

CHAPTER 9

1. See the publications of Education and World Affairs, Inc., esp., J. W. Nason et al., *The College and World Affairs* (Hazen Foundation, 1964) and *The University Looks Abroad* (New York, 1965.)
2. See W. Leys, "The Negativism of Political Goals," *The Antioch Review*, July 1968, for a discussion that is, hopefully, not too romantic.

Glossary of Indian Words

AHIMSA	Nonviolence, Noninjury
ASHRAM	Monastery, but need not have a religious significance; a place of retirement away from the people
BAPU	Literally "father"; Gandhi was known popularly as "Bapu," 'the father of the nation."
CHARKHA	Spinning Wheel
DARIDRA-NARAYANA	The poorest and lowliest people
HARTAL	Closing of shops and other business establishments as a sign of civil protest.
HIMSA	Violence, Injury
JI	As in "GandhiJI" means "Respected," "Revered."
KHADI	Handspun Cloth
MAHATMA	Great Soul, Revered
MOKSHA	Salvation, Liberation from mundane existence and suffering (in Hinduism)
NIRVANA	Salvation, Liberation from mundane existence and suffering (in Buddhism)
PANCHAYAT	A (village) Municipal Council
RAMA-RAJYA	The perfect Kingdom of Rama, a mythological king of India; Utopia
RISHI	Saint, Seer
SATYA	Truth
SATYAGRAHA	Literally "Truth Force." In common usage refers to Gandhian methods of effecting institutional changes.

SATYAGRAHI	One who practices *Satyagraha*
SHASTRAS	Sacred Scriptures
TAPAS	Sacrifice, Suffering

Index

(*Faculty members and students of Southern Illinois University are indicated by an asterisk.*)

Accreditation, 95, 102
Action, viii, ix, 4, 14, 35, 71, 97, 99, 106, 107, 109
Addams, Jane, 63
Administration. *See* Organizational problems
Ahimsa, viii, ix, 8–25, 54, 83, 85, 86, 90, 113, 116
Alienation, 76, 97–99
Alinsky, Saul, 88, 89, 130*n*8
Anarchy, 23, 55, 87, 124*n*42
Axtelle, George,* 126*n*18

Banfield, Edward, 75
Bargaining, 87, 90, 105
Bedau, Hugo, 126–27*n*3
Bergson, Henri, 81
Bhagavad-Gita, 31, 118
Blacks. *See* Negroes, American
Bondurant, Joan, 85
Brooklyn College, 92
Brownell, Baker,* 74, 75, 77, 108, 127*n*8
Buddhism, 9

Caldwell, Oliver,* 95
California, University of, 92, 93, 129*n*2
Carmichael, Stokely, 88, 89
Character. *See* Moral Education
Childs, John,* 132*n*19
Chisholm, George Brock, 63

Chomsky, Noam, 94
Christianity, 12, 37, 87, 104
Columbia University, 92
Committee on Economic Development, 73
Community, 74–77, 90, 114–17
Compromise, 22
Conflict, 5, 82–90, 104, 116
Confrontation, 91–113
Counts, George S.,* 69, 127*n*3
Crafts, 48, 70, 73–74
Crime and corrections, 84, 85, 113, 129–30*n*2
Curriculum, 48–53, 56, 58, 107

Das Gupta, A. K., x
Davis, Thomas M.,* 130*n*1
Decentralization, 40, 54, 55, 102
De Jouvenel, Bertrand. *See* Jouvenel, Bertrand de
Democracy, 36, 40–42, 92–93, 95, 127*n*5
De Tocqueville, A. *See* Tocqueville, A. de
Dewey, John, 85, 106
Discipline, 14, 26, 57, 112, 113
Dreher, Robert H.,* 129*n*2
Drop-outs, 70
Drucker, Peter, 127*n*7
Duty, 9, 11, 21, 22, 119

Education, 16, 47–62, 68–81, 82–90, 105–13, 116
Emerson, Ralph Waldo, 58, 107
Employment, 69, 73, 74
Ends and means, 9, 14, 44, 59, 85, 101

DATE DUE

3964432			
E-TOWN			
11-9-94			

Demco, Inc. 38-293